COASTAL COMPETITION

COASTAL ADVENTURES SERIES VOLUME 12

DON RICH

Library of Congress PCN Data

Rich, Don

Coastal Competition/Don Rich

Florida Refugee Press LLC

Cover by: Cover2Book.com

This is a work of fiction. Names, characters, and incidents are either the product of the author's imagination or are used fictitiously. Any resemblance to actual persons, living or dead, businesses, companies, events, or locales is purely coincidental. However, the overall familiarity with boats and water found in this book comes from the author having spent years on, under, and beside them.

Published by FLORIDA REFUGEE PRESS LLC

Crozet, VA

Copyright © 2024 by Florida Refugee Press LLC

For my wife, partner, and pal of over thirty-seven years, Victoria Tyler Rich. I'd do it all over again with you.

PROLOGUE

T*wo months ago...*

SHE SAT down in a client chair across the desk from the man. He appeared to be about ten years older than her mid to late thirties. The guy was mostly bald, with a silvery strip of hair running from just above each ear and meeting up in the back. She had mostly sandy-colored hair, though some small streaks of gray had begun to mix in.

The man hadn't stood when she came into the office, wanting to set the "I'm very busy, so get to the point" tone right up front. That, or he didn't want to let her height advantage show. At five feet, six inches tall, he was three inches shorter than her.

"Frankly, I don't understand why you asked for this meeting," he said.

"Because I think we both would love to take a shot at getting some payback from my ex-husband and his joined-at-the-hip buddy." She almost spat the words out. "That had to really chap your butt over what happened with both of those Lynnhaven and Cape Charles deals."

The man's face clouded. "Your connection to your husband was the only reason I agreed to take this meeting in the first place since you refused to tell my assistant what it was about. Would you mind telling me how I'm supposed to accomplish this payback?"

"*EX*-husband. And it's how *WE* are going to accomplish it. Together. In a partnership. We both bring different strengths to the table that will be necessary to pull this off."

The man glanced at his watch, then looked up and said, "Please get to the point."

The woman smiled, determined to take her time as she explained the details. And there were a *lot* of details. "You know those sixty acres across the road from *Mallard Cove*? I have an option to purchase them for next to nothing. They're the perfect location for a competing marina, restaurant, beach bar, and hotel. The last piece of the southern tip of the Eastern Shore of Virginia that isn't owned by the government which remains undeveloped."

He looked across the desk at her like she was completely daft. "Of *course*, I know that piece. The reason you could get it for next to nothing is because that's all it's worth...nothing. Most of it is classified as sensitive wetlands, meaning you can't touch it. I looked at it right after *Mallard Cove* was sold, wanting to build exactly what you described. But you can't, and you've wasted your money buying that option. Now, if you don't mind, I'm very busy."

"You're supposed to be smarter than this."

"*Excuse* me?"

"I always make sure that I hear every part of a proposal before I make a decision."

He said, "There's nothing to decide; that property is worthless. You should know that you can't build anything on a property that's deemed to be wetlands."

She smiled, tilting her head slightly. "Ordinarily, you would be right. Unless you could transfer credits from a mitigation bank from within the same county."

"A what?"

The smile got wider. "A *mitigation bank*. That's a process where you buy vacant farmland, strip it of its topsoil, dig it out, and flood it, creating new marshland and wildlife habitat. Every acre of the new marsh is equal to a mitigation credit, which can be used within the county where it was created. Farmland that can be bought for eighty-five hundred dollars per acre then yields credits that are worth sixty-five thousand an acre. I've already bought a couple-hundred-acre farm up off Route 13."

Now, he was intrigued, but skeptical. "There's no way in hell the Northampton Board of Supervisors will vote to allow you to do that."

"They don't have any say over it. As it stands, this can all be done 'by right.' No permits from the county are required, only approvals from the Army Corps of Engineers and the Virginia Department of Environmental Quality, which I've already obtained." She took a sheaf of paper out of her briefcase and placed it on the desk. "I'm having the equipment moved onto the farm as we speak."

The man leaned back in his chair, looking thoughtful. After a moment, he said, "It sounds like you already have this well thought out. So, why are you here? What would you need me for?"

"I need financing for the project, but the damn banks won't lend me the money because they say I don't have any development experience. This is despite my original involvement in the *Bayside Resort*, which my ex stole from me. And I've already tied up the majority of my free cash to get to this point. With your history of development, it would be easy for our partnership to obtain financing for the rest of the project. Because of this, you were the first person I considered contacting. Paybacks can be so rewarding, don't you think?" She smiled, leaning back in her own chair.

"Assuming this all checks out, I might be interested. So, what would we call our partnership?"

"How about *Shaw & Cetta Development Corporation*?"

"I like alphabetical order better: *Cetta & Shaw Development Group*." Glenn "Birddog" Cetta grinned for the first time this morning.

"That works too," said Sally Hudgins-Shaw, Casey Shaw's second ex-wife. She stuck her hand across the desk as her smile became more sinister looking. "I think it would look great on a sign directly across from the driveway at *Mallard Cove*, don't you?" She paused briefly, smiled, then asked, "So, do we have a deal?"

Cetta took her hand and nodded. "Tentatively, yes, we do. As I said, if it all checks out. And yes, that name will look great on a sign that Shaw and Murphy have to look at every day while our project gets built out. I look forward to a profitable and mutually satisfying partnership, Mrs. Shaw."

"Ms. Shaw, but call me Sally, Glenn. This is going to be a lot of fun."

1

NEW NEIGHBORS?

L *ate Friday afternoon...*

MICHAEL "MURPH" Murphy was about to turn into the driveway at the *Mallard Cove* complex when he spotted a surveyor's truck pulling out from the wooded marsh property directly across the road. Thats when he also noticed several wooden stakes on that property with surveyor's tape fluttering from their tops. These stakes were set back just beyond the roadway easement. He continued his turn into *Mallard Cove*, then pulled off to the side of the driveway, parking in the adjacent swale. Murph got out of his truck and crossed the highway, intent on finding out about those stakes. He figured it might have to do with the county maybe adding a bike lane or even a sidewalk next to US 13, but he wanted to make sure. As one of the majority partners in *Mallard Cove*, he liked keeping abreast of any changes in the area that might affect their property.

The stakes were marked as property lines and extended quite a distance. The overall road frontage of the parcel appeared to be much longer than *Mallard Cove's*. Murph followed an old dirt bike trail that led deep into the shrub-covered property, all the way back to a tiny, natural, tree-lined cut on the Chesapeake Bay. It was barely wide enough and deep enough to hold a small boat. He'd known about the trail and where it had led; it was used occasionally by fishermen who parked up by the road and walked in, so this was no surprise.

What was a surprise were some of the notations he discovered written on several of the survey stakes along the trail, as well as some of those he found farther back in the scrub. He searched as long as he could in the waning daylight before giving up and jogging back to his truck. Murph was now in a big hurry to find his wife, Lindsay, and their business partners. He drove through the *Mallard Cove* complex, past the hotel, restaurants, marina basin, and finally, past the boat dry storage barn. Ahead was a thick line of evergreens that blocked the view of what lay behind, including their security fence. He used a remote to open a gate in the fence and took the curving driveway into what was known as *Casey's Cove*.

This was a twenty-one-acre private compound owned by his friends, Casey and Dawn Shaw. Its main feature was a small, deep-water, natural basin that was where the Shaws kept their 110-foot Hargrave yacht, *Lady Dawn*, which was their floating home. After Casey and Dawn bought this property, they added numerous slips around the basin for the boats of their closest friends. This included Murph, Lindsay, and their twin-deck house barge, *On Coastal Time II*. Murph parked behind this house barge, nicknamed *OCT*. He quickly discovered that Lindsay wasn't aboard, but he knew where to look next to find her.

In warmer weather on a Friday evening, most of "the gang" would normally be hanging out at what was known as *C2*, which was short for *Cove Club*. This deck area contained a pool with a hot tub, an outdoor kitchen, a fire pit, and a guest house. However, spring had only just arrived, and it hadn't yet brought with it the warmer weather they could expect in a few weeks when the temperature would be better suited for spending time outside. Besides, Murph knew Lindsay's attention would likely be focused on another recent arrival, so he knew exactly where to look for her.

Rushing over to *Lady Dawn*, he found his wife, Lindsay, sitting with the Shaws in their yacht's comfortable salon. She was seated on the couch, smiling as she held Casey and Dawn's six-week-old daughter, Summer. Looking up at Murph, she read the concern on his face.

"What's wrong, babe?"

Murph sat next to her and looked over at Casey and Dawn. "Hey, gang. When I got back, I saw some surveyors leaving that property across the street and noticed they had installed some stakes up by the road. Those were only the beginning. I took that trail that leads back to the water and found a ton of other stakes, most of them grade stakes, marked for fill dirt."

Casey said, "That's not possible, it's a mistake. That entire property is a designated wetland. Nothing over there can ever be disturbed."

"I'm just telling you what I saw, and even worse, I found some that designated the perimeter of a huge marina basin, much bigger than ours at *Mallard Cove.*"

"Casey's right, that has to be a mistake. We all based what we were willing to invest in this property knowing it was the only available piece around that could be built on anywhere near here. Everything else is either government-owned or wetlands. There's no way anything could be disturbed, much less anything built over there. We've had our own monopoly over here as the first place you see when you get off the CBBT," Dawn said.

The CBBT stood for the Chesapeake Bay Bridge Tunnel. This seventeen-mile group of tunnels and bridges connected the Eastern Shore of Virginia, or ESVA, with the mainland at Virginia Beach. It ended opposite their property. Having the only businesses at the southern tip of the peninsula had given their group a huge advantage. If they'd had any competition in the area, it would have changed how far and fast they would have expanded their business.

They and some of their group's other partners had taken over the property a few years back when it was a mess—a defunct restaurant and docks that were literally falling in at some spots. Since then, they had turned it into one of the most successful marina properties on or near the Chesapeake Bay.

Casey said, "I wouldn't let it spoil your weekend, Murph. Like I said, it's got to be a mistake. First thing Monday, I'll run to Eastville and check with the building department. But I'm telling you, there's nothing to be concerned about. They wouldn't even let us gravel it and use it for overflow parking on holidays, or I'd have suggested we buy it a long time ago.

"If I were you, I'd be more worried about how Lindsay keeps looking at Summer, pal. She might be thinking that she wants one of her own." Casey winked at Lindsay, who smiled in return. Then he stood up, heading for the salon's bar. "What can I get you, Murph, rum or vodka? I get enough of these in you, and Summer may end up with a playmate."

Lindsay's grin grew wider at Casey's comment, especially after Murph replied, "Rum."

She said, "I'll just have a seltzer, Case..."

But little did the group know that they wouldn't have to wait until Monday for an answer about what was happening to the property across the highway. They wouldn't like what that answer would turn out to be, either.

2

BONUS PAY

4:*a.m. on Saturday...*

THE SLIPPERY TRAIL was always a challenge for the Suzuki DR-Z400S Enduro motorcycle. Built for both off-road and on-road use, it wasn't the best in either situation. Though it had the necessary lights and licenses to make it legal on Virginia's roads, the concessions that the manufacturer made for trail riding took away from its grip and performance on asphalt, which was better suited to those wider tire "crotch rockets." Similarly, when off-road, its less-than-knobby tires lacked the ability that true motocross-style tires provide in the dirt and the mud, both of which this trail had plenty of.

But despite its shortcomings, Ben Cleary handled the bike well, both on the road and now on the trail. The twenty-one-year-old had made this run a dozen times; it was like the bike knew the way by heart since he had long before memorized every twist, turn, and mud hole in the route. Because of this, he was taking the trail much faster than he should have been. The only light came from the bike's headlamp, creating a tunnel effect where the trail cut through the brush. Outside and beyond the reach of the beam was only blackness.

As he came out of one of the most radical turns, he suddenly spotted a wooden stake with some plastic ribbon dead ahead, right in the middle of the trail. Ben was able to correct slightly to try and avoid hitting the stake, but the steel rebar pin that had been driven into the ground next to it was a different subject. He leaned the bike slightly as he turned to avoid hitting the wooden stake, but the sharp edge of the metal pin's exposed top managed to catch the sidewall of his front tire, puncturing it. He tried to recover, but the now deflated tire caused the front wheel to wobble, and Ben was forced to lay the bike down on its side. He slid and bounced slightly as he hit the marshy edge of the trail; he and the bike finally came to rest in a bush.

After taking a few seconds to recover from being stunned, he began to crawl out of the bush. He pulled his right leg out from under the bike's frame, and that's when he felt the searing pain in his ankle. It had ended up under the front part of the exhaust pipe, the part that lacked a heat shield. Taking a penlight out of his pocket and shining it on his leg, he saw that some of the skin had stuck to the exhaust pipe when he freed it from under the frame. It was definitely going to need some medical attention, but this was going to have to wait. His leg wasn't his biggest concern right now; delivering the package in his backpack was, and he was only a few hundred yards away from the tiny cut where he was supposed to meet the boat.

Hiking that last bit of trail in the dark wouldn't ordinarily be that difficult, even in the darkness with only his penlight to find his way. But now his pant leg was rubbing against the raw wound, making each step agony. He stopped to roll his pant leg up, leaving the wound exposed, though if he stuck to the center of the trail with nothing to rub against it, this shouldn't be an issue.

Five minutes later, he reached the little cut. He flashed the penlight out toward the bay and heard an old two-stroke outboard crank up just offshore. Two minutes later, a grungy wooden deadrise skiff idled into the cut, and its motor shut off. A voice in the boat asked, "Where's the bike? I didn't see your light. I was gettin' worried, ain't like you ta be late."

"Blew a tire and had ta lay it down back there onna trail. Damn exhaust pipe got my leg." He flashed his light on his ankle.

"Damn, boy! Ya better get that fixed up. Everythin' around here'll get that infected, 'specially these things." The man Ben and his brother called "the Captain" used his own penlight to illuminate several plastic bushel baskets on his deck that were loaded with oysters.

"This is as close ta those an' the water as I'm gettin'. Got my cash?"

"Ain't I always? What, ya don't trust me no more?"

"Yeah, but I gotta get goin'. Now I gotta push that damn bike all th' way back."

The Captain smiled slightly in the dark, now having gained this tidbit of information. Wherever Ben and his brother produced the product was apparently within walking distance. The Cleary brothers had always been so careful not to give away any information about the location of where they cooked the crystal meth he bought from them. So damn secretive. The range of the motorcycle meant they could have been coming from anywhere on the Eastern Shore. But if Ben was going to push it home, it had to be within a few miles. Good to know. Information like that might come in handy someday.

"Here." The Captain handed a paper bag across the narrow strip of water between his boat and the shore while Ben simultaneously passed his backpack over to him. Ben now shined his penlight into the bag, counting the rolls of paper bills secured by rubber bands. The number of bills in each of the Captain's rolls was always correct, and his payments were always dead on, but it never hurt for him to see Ben double-checking.

Meanwhile, the Captain was busy emptying Ben's backpack of several quart-size plastic zip bags, each filled with white crystals and a little bit of powder, each bag weighing exactly a pound. The Captain wrapped each of the bags individually with burlap, then placed them in the bottom of empty bushel baskets before placing oysters on top of them. Each of the six one-pound bags that he'd paid five grand apiece for would net him twenty-five hundred more in profit. He'd make two delivery stops on the west side of the bay, and his total pay would be fifteen thousand bucks, not bad for a few hours' work.

He had no illusions about why he was so highly paid for such easy work, though. The physically hardest part of the gig was transferring the full oyster baskets up onto the docks. There, the distributors would load them into small, refrigerated trucks, looking like regular tidewater fishmongers. This was the perfect camouflage. But the Captain's risk was mostly in transporting the load across the open bay. He could easily be stopped, and his load checked for the oysters' sizes and point of origin. Since they came from the ocean side of the peninsula, regulations for these were a bit more lax. But still, he'd have to keep an eye out for Virginia marine resource officers.

The Cleary brothers were good at two things: cooking the best meth and being cautious. Neither of them was a user of their own product, the downfall of many who manufactured the crystals. To them, this was just an extremely high-margin product in great demand. Avoiding risk was part of their business plan, which was why they only transported it a few miles on land in Ben's backpack. In passing it off to the waterman, they avoided the cameras and the usual police presence around the CBBT highway. To them, the money that the Captain would make was simply considered the cost of insurance. He was the one who was in contact with the dealers. Neither of the brothers knew who those people were, and they never wanted to know. They didn't even know the Captain's actual name. Limiting their contact to this one person drastically reduced their exposure risk.

The Captain passed the now empty backpack over to Ben, who loaded the bag of cash into it and then slung the pack over his shoulder. The Captain killed his penlight, and from the darkness of the boat, he advised, "Best not to get caught with that cash while you're pushin' a dead bike down the side of the road. That's cop bait for sure."

"Yeah, I already thought about that. I'm gonna stash it an' come back fer it. Don't worry, I got this," Ben replied.

"That's what I get paid for, ta worry for ya. I don't want ya gettin' pinched. Wouldn' be good fer any of us."

"I GOT it," Ben said irritably. "You jus' worry 'bout you. I gotta go."

"Right. Catch ya on the radio later."

"Yeah."

The radio reference was about their use of the marine VHF radios. Cell phones with GPS installed were easily tracked by law enforcement, even when they weren't on an active call. But VHF radios were tough to pinpoint and could only be tracked when transmitting. One of the drawbacks was that they were only good for line-of-sight communication and wouldn't reach beyond the horizon. Another issue was that it was open for anyone with a similar radio to be able to listen in on their conversation. But to the Clearys, the benefits outweighed any drawbacks. They simply spoke in code and at predesignated times.

Today, when the Captain got back to the Eastern Shore after making his deliveries, he would hail a non-existent boat on a specific channel if all had gone well. The Clearys wouldn't even need to acknowledge his transmission. However, if the Captain were to get busted, that scheduled transmission would never happen. By missing the "call," they'd know there was trouble. Untraceable communication was exactly what they wanted, and unlike cell phones, there was no record of any conversations.

On the way back to the bike, Ben did a lot of thinking. He knew the Captain was right. Pushing a disabled motorcycle down the side of the road was going to attract a lot of attention, especially in these chilly, predawn hours. Northampton County deputies loved a great excuse to stop and frisk people late at night, or in this case, the predawn hours. He certainly didn't want to have to try and explain why he was carrying thirty grand in cash with him. By the time he reached the bike, he'd come up with a plan. Ben would hide the backpack off the trail in the shrub up by the highway. Then he'd walk the bike home and come back with his brother in his truck. They'd bring fishing rods with them as cover just in case they ran into anyone at the trail. He would retrieve the bag, and they'd go back home. This would work great.

An hour later, pushing the bike on the shoulder on the northbound side of the highway, Ben saw the reflection of blue strobe lights on the trees to his right. He looked back and saw a sheriff's car pulling up behind him with its lights on. Both he and the car stopped simultaneously. A big deputy in his early thirties got out and shined a flashlight in Ben's face.

"Good morning. What seems to be the trouble?"

"Ya mind not shinin' that light in my face? I can't see nothin'." When the deputy lowered the beam, Ben continued, "I hit a piece a rebar back there by *Mallard Cove*, an' it curled up an' took out mah sidewall on mah front tire. Made me run off the side of th' road, and I had ta lay it down. Now I gotta push it home."

"Where's home?"

"'Nother mile an' a half up th' road."

"Where is that rebar?"

"I threw it back inna woods so nobody else would get it inna tire."

"Where are you coming from?"

"That hotel at *Mallard Cove*. Met this little hottie at the beach bar las' night an' went back ta her room, ya know? Had ta get outta there afore she woke back up."

"Can I see your license and registration, please?" The way the deputy said it was more like a demand than a request.

It irritated Ben because he wasn't riding the bike when the deputy stopped, though he had admitted riding it. He pulled both items from his wallet and handed them over without argument.

"Wait right here."

Yeah, like I can really get on the bike and ride off, Ben thought. He was grateful that the Captain had suggested this might happen. If he'd had the backpack with him, he'd have been screwed right now because this deputy would undoubtedly have searched it.

After a couple of minutes, the deputy came back, handing Ben's items to him. The bike wasn't stolen; it was registered to Cleary, and his clean commercial license had the proper motorcycle endorsement. But something about the kid still bugged him. Maybe because the address on both his license and registration was a PO box. Or maybe it was his smarmy remark about sneaking out on the girl. The fact that the deputy had a little sister about the kid's age didn't help. He was always trying to protect her from guys like this, something she never truly appreciated.

"How'd you afford a bike like this?"

"Workin', man! Me an' my brother got a marine construction business. Fixin' seawalls an' docks, puttin' in boat lifts, stuff like that. It's why I gotta get back, so I ain't late for work."

"Okay, here's the deal: I need you to cross the road and push your bike along the other shoulder, facing the traffic. Walking with the traffic like you are makes it more likely that you could get hit from behind. At least by facing the traffic, you'd see a vehicle coming and have a chance at jumping out of the way." It wasn't like he would care if Cleary became an oily spot on the road, but he didn't want the paperwork that would come along with that.

"Yeah, okay." Ben was relieved that the deputy wasn't going to make him put it on a flatbed wrecker. Who knew how long it would take for one to get here, and the false dawn was already showing in the eastern sky. He needed to get back and retrieve the money.

"You be safe out here," the deputy said as he turned back toward his car.

Ben nodded, not that the deputy could see it. There was a crossover on the divided highway about a hundred yards ahead. With no traffic coming, he made his way across the lanes and then began pushing the bike north again. After he crossed over, he glanced back at the deputy's car. The light was on inside, and he appeared to be writing something on his computer.

Oh great, Ben thought. *I didn't wanna attract attention, an' now he's makin' notes about me.*

Ben and his older brother Greg always went out of their way to avoid getting on the radar of law enforcement. Something had changed after he'd given the deputy that made-up story about the hottie at the hotel. Exactly what, he didn't have a clue. But Greg was always telling him to stick close to the truth if he got stopped, and last summer, he *had* met a little bar fox, then had a grand old time back at her hotel room at the *Cove.* Either the deputy didn't believe his story, or he didn't like it. Probably didn't like it. If he hadn't bought it, he'd have followed up with a lot of questions. Maybe the guy was jealous over other guys gettin' laid; who knew?

Ben was jolted out of his thoughts when an oncoming caravan of several lowboys loaded with earth-moving equipment passed by in the nearest lane to him. Following close behind was a line of several large dump trucks, all of them loaded with rock and gravel. They all turned off back at that little breakfast dive.

What the hell are they doing, he thought. *Working on a Saturday? Somebody's got a big project an' a big overtime bill comin'.*

BILL BENDECK WAS WAITING in the warm cab of his pickup at the job site, watching the southbound lane for the equipment to arrive. He had been a site foreman for Shore Contour Dirtworks, LLC, for the past twenty years. He'd watched the company grow from a handful of small front-end loaders to now being the largest total site development and utilities installer on the Eastern Shore, with a huge collection of heavy equipment for every kind of dirt job imaginable.

Finally, he saw the clearance lights atop a single approaching semi. He hopped out of his truck as the driver pulled over and turned on his flashers. The driver got out, and then the two men quickly went to work unloading the big Caterpillar bulldozer on the lowboy behind the tractor.

"The other guys looked like they'd be a half hour or more behind me," the driver told Bill. "They were stopping for breakfast back at that place with th' great biscuits."

"Good, that should give me just enough time to clear some of this brush crap outta the way and make a decent spot to unload all of them, too."

Bill climbed up in the operator's seat and unloaded the machine, turning on its headlights and getting right to the job of clearing the brush. The driver of the lowboy left ten minutes later, leaving Bill working alone on-site. Five minutes after that, he spotted something in the lights of the dozer. At first, he was afraid it might have been a body or even a part of a body, but when he got down and inspected it more closely, he saw that it was only a black backpack. Opening it and then the paper bag that was inside, he recognized the familiar green color of the bills.

Glancing around, Bill was reassured that he was alone. He took the backpack over and locked it in the tool safe that was bolted into the bed of his pickup. Designed to secure expensive tools on a job site, Bill had the only key, and the backpack and its contents would now be locked safely out of sight. His mind was racing as he climbed back up in the Cat. He thought best while running a big piece of equipment like this, just as he was now.

He knew somebody had stashed that money here, so they must be planning to return for it. Unless they were dead. It was probably drug money; there was a lot of activity like that around the waterfront. And if it *was* drug money, the owner being dead wasn't so hard to believe, then they wouldn't come back around looking for it. It wasn't like some orphanage or a nonprofit would have left a pile of money here, so he wasn't taking anything from somebody who was doing good with it.

If he called the cops and turned it in, they'd likely shut the site down and send a crew out here to search for clues. It might be a day or two before they could get started again, and his boss said that they had to get as much done as possible this weekend. He said Cetta & Shaw had been willing to pay extra to make that happen. Little did they know that the double pay they'd agreed to now came with a significant bonus for Bill. All tax-free and off the books. Nope, he'd have to send his guys home if he called the cops, and that would be screwing his guys out of double pay, and there was no way he'd do that to them. In fact, he *owed* it to them not to call the cops! He thought, *Keep scraping dirt, Bill, and keep your mouth shut.* Nobody was going to be the wiser.

3

OHHH, MEXICO

T he sun was peeking over the horizon when Ben made it back home with the motorcycle. Home was the trailer he and his brother lived in on the canal bank next to their barge. This was a vacant canal on the east side of the peninsula where, years before, a group of newbie investors had planned to parcel out and sell lots on either side of the water. They were envisioning a boater's paradise that people would line up to buy into. Unfortunately, these would-be developers had underestimated how much work would be involved. They had run out of money after digging the canal, but before they could install the necessary infrastructure. In the end, they had to put the entire parcel back up for sale. Though with the huge investment needed to install the underground utilities and seawalls for such a development, there wasn't much interest in the property. Potential buyers saw it for what it was: a ditch in the swampy middle of nowhere. Without any serious buyer in sight, it was eventually abandoned, and the title reverted to the county in lieu of the back taxes.

The boys' father then picked up the property for a song at auction. It was located too far from the nearest town or grocery for a housing development, probably the largest and most damning detail the original developers had overlooked. The land around the canal wasn't the highest elevation around, either, putting it more at risk for flooding. The boys' father knew that it would probably increase in value over a few decades as towns expanded and commercial businesses moved their way, but that wouldn't happen anytime soon. He wasn't in any hurry, either, since it was a great place to base his marine construction business. The canal afforded easy access to his barge for loading materials and fuel.

The boys inherited the marine construction business after their father was killed in a car wreck not long after he bought the property. However, the business proved to be a very tough and competitive one, and without the ability and connections of their father, they couldn't keep it profitable. Competing with larger operations with more equipment and personnel was becoming harder and harder, and they were losing out on all the jobs with larger profit margins. Even after cutting back to just the two of them without any employees, they were still losing money. Shutting down the business had become their only option.

Without any income and with property taxes looming and lacking enough cash on hand to pay them, desperation set in. If he wanted to avoid the property being lost for a second time because of back taxes, Greg would need to figure out a way to make some quick cash. In a freak coincidence, he ran into Jeff Emery, a guy he knew from chemistry class back in high school ten years ago. The two of them had been the best in that class, each having real talent in this field, and had become lab partners as well as close friends. As it was with so many kids, after graduation, they drifted apart, only occasionally running into each other.

It was on one of these occasions that Jeff saw Greg again at a local dive bar. Over a few beers in a secluded corner booth and after many questions, Jeff was convinced that Greg hadn't picked up any law enforcement connections since they'd left high school. After hearing about the spot he was in—lacking enough cash to pay the taxes—Jeff offered him a short-term solution. He would agree to front Greg the money for the taxes if he would cook meth for two weeks while Jeff and his girlfriend went on a vacation to Mexico. Jeff remembered how talented Greg was back in chemistry class and knew he could easily teach him how to make the crystals.

Jeff explained about his rules about never touching his own product and treating his meth production just like any legitimate business. He'd put the distribution together and had his "lab" in an abandoned-looking trailer in the middle of his soybean field, where the strong odor from the processing would dissipate long before it could reach any of the neighboring properties.

While it was a very profitable operation, it meant Jeff had become a victim of his own success. If he wanted to keep the operation going, there could be no gap in the supply chain. He was the only "cook," not trusting his secret operation to anyone else before now. Over the past few years, he'd managed to squirrel away hundreds of thousands of dollars, yet he lacked the ability to fully enjoy any of it because he couldn't take off more than a day or two. Any longer than that, and he risked running his customers out of product. Meaning they would start looking for alternate suppliers, something he desperately needed to avoid having happen.

While Jeff and his girlfriend purposely kept a low profile, they did manage to get out and occasionally eat and drink in some of the better places on the Eastern Shore, paying in cash, of course. They would even occasionally treat themselves to a night or two at the *Bayside Resort*, but that was the extent of any time off for them. That didn't stop them from dreaming about a nice, long Mexican vacation. But without someone he could trust back on the Shore to keep things going, it was out of the question. His chance meeting with Greg solved both of their problems.

Greg turned out to be very adept at making the product and didn't have any reluctance or misgivings about what the drug would be doing to the end users. Realizing what a perfect solution he'd stumbled into, it wasn't long before Jeff and his girlfriend were winging their way south. In order to attract as little attention as possible, they charged only the bare minimum on Jeff's credit cards, no more than you'd expect a small soybean farmer to be able to afford. This meant economy-class plane tickets and a room with no view at their resort. Both of these were quickly upgraded on arrival by using cash.

Once in Mexico, bar tabs, food, and shopping were also paid for in cash. Unfortunately, spreading around that much cash attracted the attention of some of the local Mexican thugs. A day before they were scheduled to leave, the bodies of Jeff and his girlfriend were discovered in their suite at the resort, though their murders were never reported as such by the media. The Mexican authorities were serious about protecting the reputation of their tourist trade. The silent implication was that Jeff and his girlfriend were victims of drug overdoses when, in fact, they'd been tortured and finally hacked to death with machetes.

Back on the Shore, Greg was shocked when the news of the two deaths finally reached him. Thinking quickly, he realized that at some point soon, the field with the trailer would end up being sold or inherited by one of Jeff's relatives. Fortunately, none of them knew anything about Jeff's meth business. He also figured that it was likely there would be cash stashed somewhere at Jeff's house, and if enough of it was found, it could bring about questions that Greg didn't want anyone to start asking.

Maybe Jeff's relatives would be smart and not open their mouths when they found the cash, but why risk it? If they thought Jeff died as a successful soybean farmer with only what he had in the bank plus this little bit of cash, then everything would be good. But if they were to find a larger pile of cash that couldn't be explained, it could wreck their late kin's reputation and open a big can of worms.

Greg knew Jeff hadn't had any relatives or friends he had trusted to tell about the lab. Greg was it, which meant that it was his for the taking. He also knew that most people had a certain reluctance to go through the home and belongings of someone who had just been murdered. It might happen before the funerals, but probably not. Jeff's house was on the far side of the soybean field, with his nearest neighbor a quarter mile away. Greg probably would have a day or two to be able to search it before Jeff's relatives descended upon it to inventory his possessions.

Ben knew all about Greg's new job since he'd had to explain to him how he suddenly came up with the cash to save their property. So now he enlisted Ben's help in searching the farmhouse. They found over two hundred thousand dollars in cash hidden in plain sight in shoe boxes on Jeff's girlfriend's side of their bedroom closet. He left two thousand in one of the boxes to be found by the heirs. Not enough to appear sketchy, but enough to make them think that was all there was and hopefully to make them stop looking. Greg thought there should be more cash than what they found, but several additional hours of careful searching had turned up nothing. If there was more money, it must not be in the house.

Greg told Ben that he had come up with a plan for continuing the meth business and was now bringing him in as a limited partner. Since the trailer wasn't going to be a safe location for the operation much longer, they would have to move everything out and set up temporarily in the utility shed on their barge's deck. After they moved all of the equipment, they torched the trailer late that night to destroy any evidence that might have remained.

The plan was to build a new lab below the rusty steel deck of the barge. Access would be through a new hatch installed in the back of that utility shed. The brothers installed new steel bulkheads below, along with modern lab equipment. This included a new fume vent hood that sucked out the toxic fumes created during the "cook." These were expelled outside through a new stack that went up through both the deck and the shed's roof, after passing through a charcoal filter. It was an even better setup than the trailer had been, but they were setting up for a long-term operation. This wasn't the only major change for the operation; Jeff had been meeting the Captain at a commercial fishing dock on the bay side of the peninsula. But this setup felt too risky for Greg, with too many eyes around. That's when he'd come up with the current location, which the Captain also agreed made better sense.

The brothers were making as much product as Jeff had before them. With the new lab equipment, Greg was able to make an even better quality of methamphetamine. The Captain said that with this quality, he could move as much meth as Greg could make. But Greg didn't want to increase their production. Making more of the product would mean the Captain would have to add more dealers, and with each new person came increased risk. Greg said they had a good thing going, and he wasn't up for increasing their exposure. So, for the past year, things had gone along like clockwork. Until this morning.

"YOU DID *WHAT* WITH THE MONEY?" Greg Cleary yelled at his brother.

"If I'd had it with me, Greg, I'd be callin' ya from jail. Five-O stopped me on th' road while I was pushin' my bike back. He'd ah searched my backpack fer sure."

Greg stared at his younger brother as he thought about what he'd said. Ben could see he was already calming down. After a minute, Greg said, "You're probably right. I like your plan, going back with fishing rods in case anyone is around. Let's get going; we're burning daylight."

DESPITE HAVING HAD several cocktails the night before on the *Lady Dawn*, Murph hadn't slept well. The survey markers on the property across the street still had him worried. There should be no legal way that anyone would be able to do anything with that property, much less build a big marina. But then why spend the money on a surveyor? Maybe it was a scam to offload the property on some unsuspecting sucker who didn't know anything about wetlands and zoning. The more he thought about it, the more he became convinced this must be what was happening.

From his bed, he looked out the window, seeing the first rays of sunlight that were just appearing. Turning and looking over in the dim light at Lindsay sleeping so soundly next to him, he decided not to wake her. Instead, he'd slip out and have an early breakfast at the *Cove Restaurant* and bring back some breakfast for her before she woke up. They baked huge cinnamon rolls over there on Saturdays and Sundays, which were well-known, surefire, high-carbohydrate cures for any "day after" fuzziness. Like what he was experiencing right now. Not a head-splitting, full-blown hangover, just a touch of cotton mouth and acid stomach that was taking the clear edges away from what looked to be a beautiful morning outside.

After dressing quietly so as not to wake Lindsay, Murph began his walk up to the *Cove.* Just as he'd thought, the day was clear, but crisp and cool. He loved this time of year at *Mallard Cove,* even though it wasn't their most profitable time. Another two weeks and the warmer temperatures would bring more fish and tourists to the area. But for now, the majority of the boats in the *Cove's* charter boat row were floating quietly in their slips. Only Bill "Baloney" Cooper's two charter boats, *My Mahi* and the *Golden Dolphin,* had their engines cranked, with their crews ready and waiting for their charter parties to appear. Both were probably going to fish near the CBBT for tautog, the only species that was showing up in any quantity so far. The seasonal rise in water temperatures would soon change this, though.

Right before Murph was about to take the turn and head for the *Cove's* dock entrance, he spotted something yellow and black across the highway from the *Cove's* mostly empty front parking lot.

No, it can't be, he thought. *Nobody would have the balls to destroy those wetlands illegally! They would be barred from any use of the property forever from that point on.*

But there it was. He'd spotted the top of the cab of a bulldozer, which was moving back and forth, clearing off the brush and small trees that covered the property. Whoever owned the land obviously didn't care about the law or the environment. This was probably why they were working on the weekend when most government offices were closed, so there weren't any bureaucrats around to put a stop to it.

Murph now raced over to the property, darting across the highway with its sparse Saturday morning traffic. A lone pickup truck, probably the machine operator's, was parked parallel to the road by the edge of the highway. The dozer was clearing a large open space next to it, and the operator's back was to the truck. As Murph approached, he spotted a set of drawings on the open tailgate of the truck. He went over and began studying the pages, each one a bigger nightmare than the last.

What didn't make any sense was that these plans had approval seals from the US Army Corps of Engineers and the Virginia Department of Environmental Quality. And it referenced something called the Northampton Mitigation Bank. But what was really mind-blowing was the name of the owner.

"Hey! Get your ass away from my truck!" Bill Bendeck had spotted Murph looking through the drawings and was now climbing down from the cab. While he could care less about the drawings, a copy would be kept with the site's permit box anyway; he didn't want anyone snooping around his truck so close to the money. It suddenly struck him that this guy might be the one who had hidden the backpack.

Now, he became wary as well as worried. The guy was about his height, which was five feet, ten inches tall, but was a little more trim than Bill and probably ten years younger than his own forty-five. He might be able to kick the guy's ass in a fair fight, but who knew if the guy had a weapon on him. Bill thought that he sure would've if he'd known beforehand that he was going to be carrying around that much cash.

"I said, get the hell away from my truck! Are you deaf as well as dumb?"

Murph turned away from the plans and addressed Bill. "You need to stop what you're doing. These are sensitive wetlands you're illegally destroying."

Bill had closed within ten feet of Murph, now emboldened by not yet seeing any sign of a weapon. "It's legal! Your nosy ass was goin' through the drawings, so you seen the approval of the Corps and the DEQ, an' that's all we need. They approved the mitigation swap, so it don't matter what kind of land this was."

Murph was now advancing on Bill. "Screw your approvals; I'll have a judge slap an injunction on your ass Monday morning."

"Yeah? Well, by Monday morning, you'll be able to see all the way to the bay, so it won't matter, now, will it, pal."

Murph kept advancing; now he'd closed to within a few feet of Bill. "No, it still will since you aren't going to get back on that machine."

"Like hell! Who's gonna stop me, you? Bring it on, pretty boy!" He held up a pair of fists, digging in his back foot in preparation for an assault by Murph, who was about to do just that, only not the way Bill had prepared for.

~

"Aw, crap, Greg; they've got a dozer on-site already. Who does dirt work on th' weekends? Wait, it's gone! The place I left th' money's gone! They already stripped off th' brush there."

"Are you sure?"

"Positive! It was only a few feet in from th' start of th' trail! An' that ain't there no more!"

Greg pulled off the road, right behind Bendeck's pickup. As they stopped, they saw Murph fake like he was going to hit Bill with a fist. Then Bill took his first swing at Murph, who deflected it and moved inside his arc. In what looked more like a wrestler's move, Murph shoved and then kicked Bill sideways, throwing him off balance. He'd been ready for a full-frontal assault but wasn't prepared to be shoved to the side, especially so early in the fight. Murph followed up with a full body block, sending Bill the rest of the way to the ground with Murph landing on top of him, knocking out his wind, and leaving him gasping for air.

The brothers got out of the truck and hurried over to where the two men were fighting. Murph saw them approach and figured they were some of Bendeck's coworkers coming to his defense. Standing up and stepping away from a still-gasping Bill, he readied himself for a new attack. Seeing Murph pivot and now focus on them, Greg held both of his hands out, palms open toward Murph.

"Whoa, there, fella, we just came to fish, not fight. What are you two fighting about?"

Bendeck wheezed, "That crazy sumbitch attacked me for no reason!"

"I had plenty of reasons! You are illegally destroying wetlands right across from my business." Murph motioned toward *Mallard Cove* on the opposite side of the road.

Bendeck got back on his feet. "I told ya, it ain't illegal! We got the Army Corps of Engineers an' th' Department of Environmental Quality approvals, an' that's all we need! Get over it!"

With that, he shoved Murph, and the two were about to get back into it when Greg tried stepping between them. Then, they all froze as a loud police siren blared from an approaching sheriff's car. The group looked like a herd of deer caught in the headlights.

4

SHE'S BAAAACK...

The sheriff's office cruiser pulled up behind Greg's truck. A deputy got out and approached the group, asking, "What's going on here?"

Once again, Murph said, "This guy is illegally destroying wetlands."

Bendeck rolled his eyes as he shook his head. "We got all the permits we need ta do this project. Pretty boy there even looked over the plans an' saw 'em, too. I told him ta keep the hell away from my truck, an' then he came after me."

Bendeck now saw that Ben had gone over to the brush pile he'd pushed aside. Ben was circling as he peered into it, apparently looking for something, and Bendeck had a good idea what that something was. "Hey, you, get away from my burn pile!"

The deputy followed Bendeck's gaze and focused on Ben, who had just turned and was now walking back toward his brother.

"Hey! Aren't you the one who had that motorcycle with a flat tire? I stopped you up the road a while ago."

Ben nodded as he walked up. "Yeah, that was me."

The deputy now squinted as he focused on Ben. "I thought you said that you were on the way to get to some marine construction work with your brother?"

"Uh, yeah, I was. But Greg's th' boss, an' he said we oughtta go fishin' instead." He motioned toward his brother.

The deputy was taken aback. "Instead of working? Man, I wish I had those kinds of options in my work. Wait, so you came here, right across the street from *Mallard Cove*'s hotel, where you said you snuck out to get away from your one-night stand...don't you think you're taking a risk of her spotting you?"

"Yeah, well, it's where we come ta fish alla time, an' I figured she wouldn't see me through alla this brush down by my fishin' spot. 'Sides, I wore her out pretty good, so she's likely still sleepin'.'"

Murph interrupted, "Can we quit worrying about that kid's love life and focus on the *crime* here?"

Bendeck said, "Yeah, deputy, there was a crime here, an' it was that ape jumpin' me! Said he was gonna make sure I wasn't gonna get back on my machine. That's assault, an' he's trespassin' on a construction site. Ya need ta haul his ass in!"

The deputy replied, "Here's the thing: I don't know which of you started what. You two were playing patty-cake when I pulled up, so I'd have to take both of you in, not just one of you. As far as trespassing on a construction site, you'd need adequate signage defining it, which you don't have, and then I'd have to take these two in as well." He motioned to Greg and Ben.

"I'm at the end of my shift, and the paperwork for this wouldn't be worth my time, especially since the judge would likely toss this anyway." He pointed at Murph, saying, "Who are you, and how did you get here?"

"I'm Michael Murphy, and I walked across the road. I'm the majority owner of *Mallard Cove* and I live over there."

The deputy's demeanor changed a bit since he knew Murphy's business created quite a few jobs and generated a lot of tax revenue for the county. He'd heard the sheriff had some clashes with the owners, but the county supervisors had told him to cool it. So, Murphy apparently had some pull at the county offices.

"Well, Mr. Murphy, I'm going to need you to go back over to your property and stay clear of this one."

"But he's breaking the law!"

The deputy turned to Bendeck, "Where are your permits? I'd like to see them."

Bendeck grabbed the blueprints off his tailgate and showed the deputy the approval seals at the bottom of the page. "See? We're gonna be haulin' fill dirt from the Northampton Mitigation Bank. Another crew from our company is creatin' a marsh up there. It's that old soybean field a few miles up the road on the right that we've been strippin' and floodin'." He turned to some documents at the back of the plans showing the details of the so-called bank.

The deputy said, "I've never seen one of these before, and it looks like it's pretty much above my pay grade. So that'll need to get sorted out at the county offices, not here."

Murph exploded, "Which won't be until Monday, and he can do a lot of damage before then! You need to shut him down *now!*"

The deputy shook his head. "That's not something I can do, Mr. Murphy. It's out of my hands."

Bendeck grinned at Murph, "An' it's not just me. I got truckloads of rock comin' an' a bunch more equipment on the way, too. Signs'll be goin' up this mornin', an' some chain-link fence for th' new equipment yard. By Monday, ya won't recognize this place."

He'd no sooner finished talking than a couple of dump trucks loaded with baseball-sized rocks pulled up. They'd finished breakfast at the popular biscuit place up the road. Bendeck pointed at the raw dirt in the area he'd already cleared, and the first truck began maneuvering over to it to drop his load.

"Like I said," Bendeck continued, "this is a construction site, an' too dangerous for sightseers. Y'all need ta clear out now; we're fixin' ta get real busy aroun' here." That last sentence was spoken in Ben's direction.

Ben was silently glaring at Bendeck, almost positive that the site foreman had found and was now stealing their money. This idea was reinforced when he'd heard the fight started when Murphy was over by the guy's truck, where the money had most likely been stashed.

Ben's stare was starting to make Bill Bendeck's skin crawl. He was about ninety-nine percent sure that Ben was the one who had hidden the money on-site. Yet he hadn't said anything about losing a backpack here, reaffirming his belief that the money was dirty. He hoped the rest of his crew would arrive before the deputy left. The dump truck drivers would pull out after dropping their rock loads and head back to pick up more rock. Meanwhile, Bendeck would be alone on-site, unable to watch out for Murph and continue to strip the scrub at the same time. Plus, the two so-called fishermen were likely to return if they were searching for the backpack. This wasn't a good time to be alone on-site.

Adding to the confusion, a newer Mercedes SUV now pulled in behind the brothers' pickup. An attractive-looking woman in her mid to latter thirties got out, scanning the work that had been done, not looking too pleased. Then she spotted Murph, and she frowned. Murph spotted her at the same time and cursed. She walked over toward him as the foreman addressed her.

"Ma'am, you're gonna hafta leave; this is a construction site."

She looked at him like he was the village idiot. She said frostily, "I'm well aware of that since it's *my* property and project, and your company has been creating my other project, too."

"Yours?" he asked skeptically.

"Mine. I'm Sally Shaw of Cetta & Shaw Development Group. I own the Northampton Mitigation Bank on the old Emery soybean farm. In fact, I created it." She turned to face Murph, who was looking completely stunned. "Hello, Murph. Are you here to welcome me to the neighborhood?" This last part was delivered in a syrupy-sweet voice.

Finally, Murph recovered enough to say, "You! I saw Cetta on the plans but never thought you might be the 'Shaw' half."

"Aww, you sound so disappointed. Were you thinking it was Casey doing something behind your back? No, it was me, your old partner."

"You were never my partner, at least not by my choice. That only happened because you tricked Casey into marrying you. Then you made sure I left so you could try to move in on Dawn, too."

Sally smiled a fake smile. "Ah, yes, Dawn. How is our luscious redhead? Oh, right, not that you'd know since she dumped your ass and then moved right in on Casey. Yet somehow, you wormed your way back in on Casey's money and became a partner again. I guess I didn't give you enough credit at the time."

"Dawn is fine. In fact, she's better than fine; she and Casey just had their first child." Murph saw that this news had the upsetting effect he'd hoped it would. "You have it wrong. *Mallard Cove* was mine; I bought it with my own money and then I invited them into the project. I earned the money to buy this, by the way. I didn't lay down on my back and screw somebody for it like you did. Then Casey asked me to come in with them on their other projects."

"Casey must've been hard up for laborers."

"Nope. We contract everything out. I'm more in charge of counting all the money we're making, and it's a lot of work! Such a shame you aren't still with us to share in it. Wait, who am I kidding? No, it's not!"

"Well, enjoy it while it lasts because everybody will forget about dusty old *Mallard Cove* when my project opens. My *Southern Shores* complex will be the new, happening place."

Until now, the four other people had been silently watching this somewhat heated exchange. But Bendeck spoke up. "Excuse me, ma'am, but I gotta get ta work on this property if ya wanna keep yer project on schedule. An' your friend here wanted ta shut me down an' get in my way."

Sally smiled. "Oh, is that so? Then, in that case, let me help you, and he's definitely not my 'friend.' Murphy, you're trespassing. Get your ass off my property, and keep it off! Officer, if he doesn't leave immediately, please arrest him. Or, shoot him. It's your call."

The lawman ignored that last part. "It's 'Deputy,' ma'am. But Mr. Murphy, you do need to do as the lady says and leave the property."

"Deputy, you've got it all wrong. No way in hell is that...bitch...a 'lady.' But I'm going, at least for now. And I'll see your ass in court,

Sally, when I get this shut down permanently and force you to return this land back to the way it was." He turned and began crossing the highway.

Sally called after him, "I'm looking forward to watching you spend your money on lawyers when you've got no case. Or is it Casey's money that you'll be spending? Not that it matters to me; I'll gladly make either or both of you waste your cash. You are about to get a very expensive education."

Bendeck now turned toward Greg and Ben. "Y'all need ta leave, too. An' you're gonna hafta find another spot ta fish. From now until it's finished, only construction crews'll be allowed on this property."

Greg said, "I got it, and we won't be back."

Ben silently glared at the man, unnerving him.

Bendeck swallowed, more sure than ever now that the backpack had come from those two. He watched as they went back to their truck and drove off.

The deputy said, "I love it when things end peacefully and without extra paperwork at the end of my shift. Y'all have a great day." Nodding at Sally, he climbed into his cruiser and drove away as the line of heavy equipment began to arrive.

CASEY WAS SITTING OUTSIDE at the table on the aft deck of *Lady Dawn* when he saw Murph quickly approaching the yacht. Then Murph glanced up and spotted him. Casey said, "Hey, Murph. I'm just finishing breakfast, c'mon aboard."

As Murph got closer, Casey could see that he was frowning, and his jaw was set. Casey waved him aboard and then motioned to a chair next to him. "Good morning, Murph; Dawn's still asleep. She was up several times last night to breastfeed Summer, so I decided to eat by myself out here and not disturb her. Do you want some coffee?"

Murph sat down, now scowling as he did. "What? Coffee? Uh, yeah, sure, thanks." He nodded at the steward, Andrea, who went back into the galley for his cup. Looking at Casey, Murph said, "We have a big problem. Sally's back and has teamed up with 'Birddog' Cetta, and they're going to build a big marina with restaurants and a hotel right across the street."

Casey looked confused. "Sally who?"

"I'm talking about your ex-wife—that Sally. That's what all those survey markers are for. She's developing the other half of the peninsula's southern tip with Cetta, and they're planning to compete with us. She's calling it *Southern Shores.*"

"That's not possible, Murph. Like I told you, all that property across the street is marshland and can't be touched."

"Right, it shouldn't be able to be, but it is. They're unloading bulldozers now as we speak! They've already cleared a big spot for an equipment corral and plan to have all the vegetation stripped by Monday. Sally said she created a mitigation bank up the road, which somehow lets her and Cetta develop wetlands. The Corps of Engineers and the VDEQ have already signed off on it; supposedly, those are all the approvals that are needed. But that can't be right, can it?"

Casey was stunned. "Sally. Sally Hudgins. And Glenn Cetta." He shook his head in disbelief. "I never thought I would hear those two would be working together, though they both hate us. A mitigation bank, you say?" He opened his laptop and began to type something. After a few seconds, he stopped, apparently focusing on one page. A minute later, he looked up at a silent Murph. Casey now had his worried face on.

"A mitigation bank thing is something new that I hadn't heard of before. Apparently, there aren't many of them around the country yet. The gist of it is that anyone can create a new marshland and then partner with an environmental conservation group to put it in a conservation easement, creating negotiable credits for every flooded acre that they can either swap for their own properties or sell outright. They're worth a fortune compared to the farmland they're replacing.

"If it's the parcel I'm thinking of, that huge old soybean field up next to the highway they've been working on north of here, it's much larger than that piece across the road. They'll have a lot of those credits left over. I don't like the concept, though I've got to give her credit for originality. According to what I'm reading here, those credits are going for a hundred grand plus per acre. The farmland isn't even worth ten grand an acre; then there's the cost of having it stripped and dug out. You're still spending less than twenty percent of that new value."

"Jeez, Case, you sound like you admire this move she's pulling on us."

Andrea reappeared with Murph's coffee and a warmup for Casey's, then cleared the empty plates and disappeared back into the cabin. Casey took a sip, then answered Murph. "Don't get me wrong, I neither admire nor appreciate what she's pulling. Unfortunately, from what I'm reading here, I don't think we are going to have much in the way of any recourse. It's freaking brilliant. Shady, but brilliant."

"So, what are we going to do about it?" Murph was exasperated.

"Well, I'm going to finish my coffee, then I'll take a ride up there and see for myself. Then, I'm going to come back here and check to see if there's any other farmland around ESVA for sale."

"What? You said it was shady!"

"Right. But if we get all the farmland that's for sale in Northampton and Accormack counties tied up under contract with closing dates that are way out, it gives us time to push for a new law prohibiting this 'bank' idea. Then, we either buy the land for farming or cancel the deal. If we don't do this, ESVA is going to become a manufactured swamp, with those credits being used for projects all over the coast of the Chesapeake. That's not what we want to see happen. We've got to get this stopped."

GREG AND BEN returned to the barge, where Ben asked his brother, "What about meetin' the Captain from now on? Can't do it there no more, so we gotta come up with a new place."

"I'm already ahead of you, little brother. We're going to use the tug and meet him out on the water in the Virginia Inside Passage. There isn't a lot of traffic out there, and we can meet him just before sunup, off of Albury's Boat Works. I don't want him to know where we are based, though the tug might give that away, but I don't know any other place that would be private enough. We'll need to take the business signs off the tug; we can make the exchanges in the wheelhouse. We've been doing business with him long enough to have built a little trust between us."

"Yeah, I guess that'd work." But Ben still didn't sound convinced.

"You know a better place?" Greg asked.

"I guess not."

"Then go ahead and strip those signs off the tug. We need to get ready well ahead of time in case he wants to meet and check out the new spot. He should be checking in a few hours from now, and we need to be all set."

"Ah'll take care of it."

5

TRESPASSERS

Casey and Murph rode to the construction site in Casey's six-seat ATV, and what Casey saw happening there almost made him sick. Then he spotted Sally sitting in a camp chair under a portable tent beside her car. She was focused on what was happening to the property.

The noise of the six large track loaders and bulldozers stripping off the underbrush covered the pair's arrival. The machines made short work of the vegetation, pushing it into a few large burn piles.

Casey walked up behind her and said loudly, "Hello, Sally."

Sally shot up and out of her chair, spinning around to face Casey as she did. "Jesus, Casey, you scared the crap out of me!" At six feet tall, Casey was three inches taller than Sally, and in his middle forties, he was not quite a decade older than her.

Murph muttered, "It's a shame it didn't give you a heart attack."

Sally glared at him. "What did you just say?"

Before Murph could repeat it, Casey said, "Never mind him; what the hell are you doing here?"

Her sickly-sweet voice was back. "Whatever do you mean, Casey? I'm just out to make a buck, the same as you. And I'm doing what you taught me. You said, 'Never reinvent the wheel if you don't have to.'

Well, you and knucklehead"—she motioned to Murph—"have done a decent job revamping the old *Mallard Cove* property and leading the way down here. Now, Glenn and I will take this property one step further with an even bigger marina, more and bigger beach bars, restaurants, and a bigger hotel. *Southern Shores* will be the gem of the Eastern Shore!"

"But it's not just a property, Sally; it's a marsh and an estuary—home to many animals before you started destroying it."

"And I'm building a larger, better marsh for them up the road. Are you starting to see a pattern here? Larger and better, like what we're doing with our facilities here. Remember that old song? 'Anything you can do, I can do better...' And that's exactly what I intend to do."

"You're going to overbuild, and then there won't be enough business for either of us at this end of the Shore. We'll be fighting over the same customers."

Sally smirked. "Afraid of a little competition, Casey?"

"I'm just saying that you need to be careful. We'll be fine with *Mallard Cove* since we don't have a lot of debt, but you are starting out with a huge overhead. You're making things tough on yourself right out of the gate."

"Why don't you worry about yourself, Casey? It's what you've always done best. It's pitiful, really, seeing you crawling over here, scared that my partner and I will take all of your business, but making it sound like you're being nice and trying to look out for me."

"So, it sounds like this is more personal than about business."

"I'm mixing business with pleasure in this case. You two enjoy your last season of being a monopoly on the southern tip of the Shore because next season, you'll be sucking sand after we open. And you've got some nerve talking about destroying stuff when you've developed acres and acres of land both across the street and elsewhere."

"Almost everything we've developed was done on properties that had already been cleared long before we bought them. But this was a pristine habitat!"

"Which my mitigation bank will replace, acre for acre, as I said.

Now, I've wasted enough time talking to you. Get the hell off my property and stay off it, both of you!"

AFTER THEY CROSSED BACK over the highway, Casey said, "Those two are absolutely going to kill all the business for everybody."

Murph replied, "I thought you were kidding, just trying to worry her."

"No, I'm the one who's worried. Did you see how far that property line goes? That place will be twice as large as *Mallard Cove*. Think about trying to make a profit with only half the number of customers that we currently have."

Murph now looked worried. "You really think it'll be that bad?"

Casey nodded. "I do. Fortunately for us, we have income from our other properties to help keep us afloat until Sally's project implodes. Cetta has had to sell most of his other properties. It turns out he's good at finding and rehabbing buildings but not so good at running the businesses that go into them. On the other hand, Sally is good at running a hospitality business. But you need to have enough of a customer base to support your business. There's no way they could have had a market survey done of this area. If they had, they'd do something else with that property instead of merely copying us."

"We've gotta get an injunction against them, Case. Get them to cease and desist before it's too late for all the animals that depend on that property."

"You won't be able to do that until Monday at the earliest, Murph. That property doesn't have until Monday, at the rate they're moving."

"Yeah? Well, we'll see about that."

HALF AN HOUR LATER, aboard *OCT*, Lindsay walked into the galley and found Murph sitting in the breakfast nook. He was staring off into space with an untouched cinnamon bun and a cup of coffee in front of him.

"Good morning, sunshine. Are we going to fight over that one bun?" Somehow, her still-sleepy eyes still managed to twinkle as she ribbed him.

"Huh? Oh, nope, yours is over there, under the heat lamp."

She turned and looked at the stainless-steel shelf under the stove's exhaust hood. Bathing in the red light of an overhead heat lamp was the twin of Murph's cinnamon bun. She grabbed the warm plate with a potholder after she poured herself a cup of coffee. Sitting across from Murph, she noticed that his focus hadn't changed. "Are you okay?"

"Hmm? Oh, kinda." He told her what he'd seen and about Casey's conversation with Sally.

"Casey's that certain about how much it will affect our business?" Lindsay asked.

"Yeah, and I think he's right. There are things we can do to counter it, but the better course of action is going to be to get an injunction slapped on them first thing Monday morning. But by then, that property will already have been ruined. Though we might be able to force them to put it back the way it was. But if we can't, and they keep moving forward with their plan, it could wreck us.

"Casey talked about having the income from the other properties to carry us until the time that Cetta & Shaw implodes, but for us, it won't be enough. Since we have a big personal bank loan that we used to buy in on those other properties, we could be in real trouble if it gets called. One of the provisions of the loan is that we have to maintain a minimum income stream from *Mallard Cove* until the new Lynnhaven and Cape Charles properties come online, and that will probably happen about the time Sally's project does. It's likely to be close. If our loan gets called, we're screwed."

Lindsay said, "Let's go over there. I want to see it for myself."

"Not a great idea, Linds. Sally would love nothing better than to have me hauled off to jail for trespassing since I've been warned to stay off her property twice now."

"She can't do that if we're on our own boat, babe." Lindsay smiled and raised one eyebrow.

Murph looked thoughtful. "I like the way you think. That foreman said he expected them to break through to the bay soon. They'll have to clear the property lines first to install a silt fence." This low-profile plastic ribbon only allowed water to pass through it, keeping all the loose dirt, mud, and sand on the property.

"Sounds logical. Now, eat up, and I call dibs on the helm!" Lindsay loved any excuse to get out on the water, especially when she was the one running the boat. *LNZ II* was their vintage thirty-one-foot Contender center console boat with twin outboard motors, which was a great and stable platform for fishing and cruising, both of which were exactly what Lindsay had in mind for the day.

FROM THEIR POSITION idling about thirty yards out, parallel to the shoreline, Murph and Lindsay had a great view of what was happening on the job site. The machines had divided into two groups, one at the north property line and another at the peninsula's southwestern tip. They were using their brush rakes to push the scrub into large piles toward the middle of the property, where it all would be burned. At the rate that the swarm of tracked machines was working, if the property weren't all cleared by Monday morning, it would be really close.

"Wow. You weren't kidding when you said it's double the size of our property," Lindsay said. At the far north end, a bulldozer had made it all the way from the highway down to the beach, giving the pair a reference point to approximate the size of the property.

"It looks even larger from the water. Casey was right; this isn't good. Sally's place is massive compared to ours. We're gonna be so screwed," Murph said.

"He's also right about there being nothing we can do about it until Monday, babe, so there's no sense worrying about it." She reached for the throttles, pushing both forward until the boat reached cruising speed, heading over to one of the small rock islands that were part of the tunnel ends fo the CBBT. She hopped up and sat on top of the leaning post, bending forward over the helm.

"Hey! Where the hell are we going, Linds?"

"Away from here. You won't be able to relax today until we're out of sight of Sally's nightmare. I need to get your mind off this."

Realizing the truth in that statement, again Murph asked, "But where are we going?"

"First, a little tautog fishing at the rock islands. Then, to Gwynn's Island for lunch at *Bay Breeze*. My treat."

"I knew I married you for a reason."

She gave him a wry smile; "I thought you married me for the sex."

"Yeah, well, it's great sex, and that's a bonus, but you make great sense, too."

"And don't you forget it!"

"It's not likely that you'd let me."

"Damn straight, babe."

DAWN EMERGED from the cabin's central stairwell. Even after waking up numerous times last night to feed Summer, she still looked stunning this morning. Her long red hair was pushed back over her shoulders, and she was very tall, only an inch shy of her husband's six feet.

Summer was cradled in her mother's arms, her short wisps of red hair and blue eyes matching Dawn's. She took her over to Casey, handing her off to Daddy while she went in search of something for breakfast. A few minutes later, she returned with an English muffin and some coffee. As she returned, she looked out through the salon's windows and across the water of *Casey's Cove*. She sat next to Casey on a couch.

"Looks like *LNZ II* is out."

"Oh? I hadn't noticed. But that's a good thing after the morning that Murph and I had." Casey went on to explain what was happening across the street. "Murph didn't take it too well when I told him how much it was likely to impact our business here."

"Well, we'll need to anticipate the effect it will have and staff appropriately next season until things rebound. We should be okay, especially with *Bayside*, our Florida properties, plus Lynnhaven and Cape Charles coming online in a year or so. We still have this upcoming season for *Mallard Cove*. You know that old saying: 'Worry is interest on a debt that you may never have to pay.'"

Casey nodded. "Tell Murph that. I know he stretched to buy into our recent projects. With he and Lindsay being the largest shareholders in *Mallard Cove*, it's their main source of income. Since they aren't involved in *Bayside*, until those other properties start bringing in cash, they might be in trouble."

"He told you that?"

"Not in so many words, but I could read it on his face. He looked panicked."

Dawn leaned back on the couch and took a long sip of coffee. Her history with Murph was complicated, to say the least. A few years earlier, she had been engaged to him. But during a rough patch in their relationship, he'd found Lindsay, who knew nothing about Dawn. Sally seized the opportunity to drive a wedge between the two even further, as well as one between Murph and Casey. She had pushed Casey to cash Murph out of *Bayside* before it became profitable. Today, his shares would have been worth many multiples of what he'd been paid for them back then. Even more importantly, they would have given him a steady income stream today.

Sally overplayed her hand at that point, making a play for Dawn, but instead, she found herself getting thrown out of Casey's life and business. When the dust settled, Casey was with Dawn, and after a relentless pursuit of Lindsay, Murph and she ended up together. The two had become the hottest sports fishing crew around, winning several high-dollar tournaments. It was at these tournaments that the two couples kept running into each other. During a rainy, alcohol-soaked celebration after Dawn and Murph won the richest billfish tournament on the East Coast, Dawn and Lindsay became friends as

Casey and Murph rekindled their friendship. Dawn decided that her new friendship with Lindsay was worth the cost of putting up with Murph being around.

At this point, Murph told Casey about his plan to buy *Mallard Cove* and rehab the property slowly over a period of years. This extended timeframe was necessary because they had used their last dime to purchase the property. Casey saw the opportunities the property presented but realized this all needed to happen much faster to maximize the profit potential. He soon talked Murph into letting him and his group of investors buy in with him and Lindsay, bringing with them the access to capital that would be needed.

Over the past couple of years, Dawn and Murph had entered into an unspoken truce: they had become casual friends again for the sake of their spouses. Dawn knew that if Murph and Lindsay got in a bind, she and Casey would come to their aid. She also knew that Murph was too stubborn and too proud to accept anything that appeared to be charity. If it came down to this, she and Casey would have to figure out how to help the pair without bruising Murph's pride. She glanced over at Casey, who had been alternating glances between her and their daughter. Dawn could read on his face that he knew exactly what she was thinking.

Finally, she said, "We'll need to help them if it comes to that."

He nodded. "Yeah. They'd both do the same if situations were reversed."

"I know that. Plus, there's more to the story I haven't told you, and Lindsay hasn't even told Murph yet. After I kidded her about wanting to have a baby, too, she told me in confidence that she just found out she was pregnant. She had planned to spring it on Murph at the perfect point this weekend, but that was before he came home so upset about Sally's project."

Casey was stunned. "Oh, wow. I had been kidding last night about needing a playmate for Summer. But that explains why Lindsay stuck to soda."

Casey stared off into space as the timing of things now hit him. Lindsay would be giving birth a few months before *Mallard Cove* would be looking at a very challenging season. The timing of things couldn't be worse from an economic point of view. But Casey was rapidly learning how much of a blessing kids could be. He'd already learned that if you held off until the so-called perfect moment to get pregnant, that time might never come. He thought of that old saying: "Foolish mortals make plans, and God laughs."

$\approx$

"THIS WAS A GREAT IDEA; THANKS, LINDS." The pair had just finished a relaxed and delicious lunch at *Bay Breeze*, a restaurant on the mainland side of tiny Gwynn's Island, across the water from Hudgins, Virginia. The long run across the bay had been worth it.

Lindsay smiled, happy that Murph had gotten his mind off what Sally Shaw was doing on the opposite side of the bay. "I'm glad you enjoyed it, but we're far from done. I thought that maybe we could troll a bit back across the bay and see if there aren't some early-season bluefish around we can add to those tautogs we caught earlier. I heard someone say that they were already coming up the coast."

"I like the way you think! Throw in some beer for me at the cleaning table, and I'll clean all we can catch."

"Don't sharpen your fillet knife just yet. If we can find some blues, you'll need to earn your keep by catching a few."

6

CHANGE OF PLAN

Ben and Greg met the Captain at the old dock rendezvous spot on the west side of the peninsula. When the Captain had made the usual call to the nonexistent boat, he'd been alarmed to hear Greg respond, telling him he'd meet the deadrise at the dock. Half an hour later, as he cautiously approached and pulled his boat alongside the pier, both brothers climbed aboard. The Captain shifted into reverse, backing out before steering toward the center of the bay, where they would have the privacy they'd need for their conversation.

The Captain didn't like any changes to their routine and was very concerned. "What's so important that we had ta meet?" he asked.

Greg replied, "Head for the usual meeting place, and we'll explain along the way." As the Captain brought the boat up to cruising speed, Greg began telling him about what was happening to the property. Then he told him about how they had a new plan for making their exchanges. When they got offshore of the meeting spot, the Captain was shocked to see how much it had changed in just a few short hours. He continued on around the southern tip of the peninsula, past *Mallard Cove,* then turning up into the Virginia Inside Passage and past *Casey's Cove* in a section of the VIP known as "the ditch." A few miles later, they were at the new rendezvous point, not far from the brothers' canal. The Captain approved.

"This'll work even better'n the old spot. This way, I'll keep goin' after I round the point like I had just picked up mah oysters and was headed ta the west side ah th' bay, lookin' more normal. There's less traffic over here ta spot us anyway." The Coast Guard had stopped maintaining the navigational aids for the Inside Passage a few years back, citing the dwindling amount of traffic and the high cost of dredging and channel marker maintenance. The few existing markers were now privately placed and maintained. "Nobody'll question ah deadrise out workin' aroun' here just before dawn."

Greg nodded. "Another plus to this new plan."

The Captain said to Ben, "Good thing you got that money outta there before they started scrapin'."

Ben frowned and looked down at the deck. "Yeah, about that…"

"Ya *did* get that outta there in time, right?" Now, alarm bells were starting to go off in the Captain's head.

"Not 'xactly." Ben sheepishly retold the story of hiding the money, getting stopped on the side of the road, and eventually going back. Arriving to find the site already cleared and the foreman in a fight with the owner of *Mallard Cove*, then getting yelled at for looking through the brush pile.

The Captain said, "So, yer thinkin' that foreman's got the cash, eh?"

Ben nodded. "Yeah, an' he told th' cop he got pissed when that other guy was lookin' aroun' his truck."

The Captain shook his head. "That ain't good. He's gotta figger you fer havin' had that cash, an' that it ain't kosher. 'Specially since ya didn't say nothin' ta him about it, not askin' if he'd ah seen it. Nah, that ain't good at all."

Greg said, "It's probably best to just drop it. He can't say anything about it, and he can't flash it around. He seemed smart enough to know that."

"Yeah, well, I'm glad it's yer thirty grand an' not mine. I wouldna been so quick ta jus' give up an' lose it."

"Pushing the issue would get people asking questions that I don't want, er, make that *we* don't want to get asked. Keeping our operation going is worth a lot more than thirty thousand bucks," Greg said.

The Captain nodded slowly. "I guess yer right. But hey, are ya sure ya still don' wanna increase yer production ah bit? Make up fer that lost cash?"

Greg remained silent while he considered it. Finally, he asked, "Can you get rid of it with the crew you've got without having to add any new people into the mix?"

The Captain nodded. "Yep. Mah guys were bitchin' 'bout not gettin' enough product, an' I don' wanna lose any of 'em. They're good, an' they know how ta keep their mouths shut." He was lying, of course. He knew of a dealer that was looking for additional sources of supply. In fact, he'd already been approached by him, though the guy made him nervous.

Greg glanced at Ben, and he could see that his brother was excited over the idea of making up for the lost cash and having the potential of added income after that. He looked at the Captain and said, "Okay. We can go up to eight pounds and forty grand per shipment if your guys can handle it."

"No sweat. That'll getcha yer money back real quick. Meantime, ya wanna steer clear ah that foreman fella. He ain't likely ta tell anybody anythin', but ya can't be too sure, knowwhatImean?"

That irritated Greg. "Of course we do. And you keep an eye out so none of your guys get popped and try to trade up information for a lighter sentence."

"Hey! These're mah guys yer talkin' about. So, don't worry 'bout mah end ah th' deal. We good? Ah got lots ta do this afternoon." Without waiting for an answer, the Captain took another look around at their location and shoved the throttle forward, marking the end of their conversation.

〰

MURPH WAS at the fish cleaning table at the *Cove Club*. Casey and Dawn had built *C2* to give them and their liveaboard friends access to the amenities their boats lacked. This included an elaborate outdoor kitchen, a stone fire pit, a hot tub and swimming pool, a helipad, and a seaplane ramp leading down into the Virginia Inside Passage. There was also a clubhouse with dressing rooms, a sauna, a pool table, a big-screen TV, and a guest bedroom.

Even with all the amenities Casey and Dawn had available on *Lady Dawn*, *C2* offered a lot of otherwise unavailable options. For instance, no matter how large your yacht was, a pool table wasn't something you could have, and it was one of Casey's favorite games.

Like everything about *C2*, the fish cleaning table was first class. It was custom-built with an anodized aluminum frame, a fiberglass table with storage drawers, and a hardtop with built-in overhead LED lights. In almost three decades of being around boats and marinas, Murph had never seen a nicer setup. Then again, he'd had a hand in designing it with Casey.

Murph was starting to clean the handful of bluefish piled on the table. They'd lucked into these early arrivers about halfway back across the bay. He wanted to get these cleaned first because he had already started the smoker, and these fillets would take two hours or longer to smoke. Murph was using natural lump charcoal along with orangewood chips from a citrus farmer in Florida that Casey knew. Orangewood was the best for smoking fish, or for most lighter-colored proteins, for that matter. It had a milder, sweeter smoke than many other woods. These bluefish were destined for a batch of the so-called "Chesapeake Crack," a fabulous smoked fish dip that Casey had originally concocted. The smoke from the cooker was already drifting over toward *Epilogue*, Sandy Morgan's trawler. Because of this, Murph knew it wouldn't be long before he'd have company, both the two-footed and four-pawed variety.

"Here you go, babe. I've got it all mixed together, and I'm letting the flavors mingle." Lindsay walked up, having made a special mustard, pepper, lemon, and mayonnaise-based mixture that each fillet would be slathered with before going into the smoker. The mayonnaise kept the fish from getting too dry while also helping neutralize the strong bluefish flavor. The mustard and pepper added spice and a slight bit of heat. "Uh-oh. Furry beggar at nine o'clock!"

KC Shaw, Sandy's boat cat, had spotted Murph at the cleaning table and was now inbound to collect the "cat tax," a small portion of all of the fish that got cleaned. KC was no ordinary house cat, and that wasn't just because he lived aboard instead of onshore. He was about sixteen inches high, tall enough for him to be nicknamed "Stretch." He's an Ocracat, one of the feral cats that were born each year on Ocracoke Island, the southernmost inhabited island on North Carolina's Outer Banks.

The famous pirate, Blackbeard, had loved spending time on Ocracoke, and it was there that he met his end in a battle with British mercenaries. Among the legends that came out of that historic day, there was one about Blackbeard's two ship cats being thrown overboard by the mercenaries after that final battle. Supposedly, these cats were left to their own devices to try and live out their days. From this day and for the next three hundred years, Ocracoke's cat population would grow exponentially. That was, up until the point where a group was formed to address this issue by trapping, spaying, and neutering as many members of the feral colonies as possible. Many of the kittens that were then born in the wild were captured and transported over to the mainland, where they were adopted. KC had stayed on the island but had no takers for a "forever home." With no other option, he was turned back out, living under the deck at one of the local stores. That was, until one fateful day, when he met Sandy.

KC was named for Casey, who had originally suggested that Sandy stop at Ocracoke on a trip leg while heading down to Florida a few years ago. The cat had followed Sandy back to *Epilogue* and had refused to leave his side except for occasionally venturing ashore to relieve himself. Sandy, a bestselling novelist, was also a widower who found the cat to be good company without needing constant attention. He usually spent his days within sight of Sandy, wherever he happened to be writing—inside during the colder months or out on the covered back deck when it was warmer.

This afternoon, KC's dark gray and black tabby-marked fur gleamed in the sun as he approached Murph and his pile of bluefish and tautog. The cat was eying Murph's closest leg, considering using it as a scratching post in order to gain his attention. But things never got that far today. Murph addressed the approaching cat: "C'mere, KC, I set aside a pile for you."

Murph dangled several pieces, one at a time, which KC happily took out of his fingers and devoured. After he was finished, Lindsay handed Murph an opened bottle of beer, though she was having a soda. She sat in a lounge chair, and then KC jumped up and settled in with her in her lap, his signal that he was ready to be petted. She happily obliged.

"Are you making a batch of 'Crack'?" The person asking was KC's boatmate, Sandy, who had appeared from behind the boathouse that was between *Epilogue* and *C2*. Sandy was in his mid-sixties, about five feet, nine inches tall with longish graying hair, a scruffy beard, and a small gold circle earring in his left ear.

Murph nodded. "First bluefish of the season, but no mahi nor mackerel to add into the mix, unfortunately. Probably next month."

"That's okay, so long as you're making plenty of this single variety dip now. Your smoke reached out and grabbed me over on my boat. That can make a man thirsty, if you know what I mean."

Murph chuckled. "Riiight, but nothing that a beer or two can't cure, I'd bet. But don't tell me, let me guess; you're 'fresh out' of beer."

"Not really, but I *do* like drinking yours instead of mine!" Then he noticed Lindsay and the cat. "Want a beer, Lindsay? Your husband is buying."

She smiled, "No. Thanks, though, Sandy."

"Somebody say that Murph is buyin' th' beer?" The voice belonged to Captain Bill "Baloney" Cooper, who was approaching from the opposite direction as Sandy. Baloney was in his mid-fifties, about five feet, five inches tall, but his voice made up for any short-comings in his height. With a thick New Jersey accent that he thought he lost years ago, he was loud enough to be heard anywhere within sight. The running joke around the marina was that he'd wasted his money installing a VHF radio on his boat since those were only good for line-of-sight communication, and his loud voice carried just as far.

Baloney lived aboard a sixty-foot Merritt sportfisherman named *Dorado*. It was straight across the basin from Murph and Lindsay's houseboat in a slip that Casey had recently installed specifically for him. This is where he was coming from, aiming to meet up with the others at *C2*.

Baloney owned those two charter boats, the *Golden Dolphin* and *My Mahi*, that were docked by the *Mallard Cove* restaurant. But his main source of income these days was the highly-rated cable show *Tuna Hunters*, which was filmed at *Mallard Cove*. As the most popular star of the show, he now earned somewhere in the low seven figures annually. Before signing up for the show, he'd made a decent living by chartering his two boats, but it was nowhere close to this much.

Baloney's quirky personality translated well to TV. Quirky in that he always had a cigar in his mouth, though it was only lit when he was out on a boat. The rest of the time, it was more like a barometer of his mood. When he was mad or agitated, the cigar would rapidly swap sides in his mouth, seemingly all by itself. Back when he lived aboard and fished on the *Golden Dolphin*, when he was returning to the dock, he would signal that they'd caught a wahoo by running a black brassiere up the outrigger line. And even though he no longer ran that boat, every Christmas season, he still put an inflatable Santa up in the tuna tower with an empty beer can in its hand. He was that kind of quirky.

One more thing about Baloney: he loved beer—other people's beer. He and Sandy would argue over a bar tab every time, not because they both wanted to pay it, but exactly the opposite. And since Sandy was the first one of the pair to bum a beer off of Murph today, it meant he was also going to be the most territorial about them. This was despite the fact that, in reality, of course, they all belonged to Murph, who had paid for them. Not that this mattered to either of his beer-mooching friends.

"No, Gilligan, he didn't say that he was buying *you* one!" Sandy knew calling Cooper "Gilligan" would irritate him, which was precisely why he did so, of course.

"I told ya ta quit callin' me that, ya hack! Now, do something useful an' pass me a beer."

Sandy grinned and pulled out two beers from Murph's cooler, handing one to Baloney. As he did so, over his friend's shoulder, he spotted an old open deadrise skiff passing by *C2* in the Virginia Inside Passage. The loud noise coming from the outboard motor unmistakably identified it as an older two-stroke engine. Sandy wondered, "Where the heck would that guy have found a two-stroke engine, a museum?"

Baloney grabbed the beer and then turned in the direction from which the noise was coming. "Looks like the boat's newer'n th' engine, and that ain't sayin' much. Prolly got it for nothin' an' fixed it up."

Sandy squinted as he watched it pass. "Were you talking about the boat or the motor?"

"Yes," Baloney replied, and the two men chuckled.

This caused Murph to look up from his work at the cleaning table, now focusing on the skiff and its occupants. "Hey! I know two of those guys. At least, I kinda met them this morning across the street. They're brothers who supposedly have a marine construction business. But they said they were going surf fishing," Murph said.

"Looks like they ran into a friend with a boat," Sandy commented.

"Beats bein' stuck onna beach, ya hack. I'd rather be out onna boat any day, even that noisy scow."

"That is something we can agree on, Gilligan. It does indeed."

Murph now refocused on cleaning the fish. He wanted to get it all done as quickly as he could. He still had to mix the fish into the base mixture after it was smoked and cooled. Fortunately, this time of the year, the temperature really started to drop after the sun set, making the job a bit faster by helping to cool the smoked fillets after they came out. And then he still had something to do before dinner.

7

THE FILTER FAIRY

E*arly morning at Casey's Cove...*

THEIR STATEROOM WAS SLOWLY GETTING BRIGHTER as the sun finally rose above the horizon. Murph looked at Lindsay's face while she was still sleeping, taking in every detail. He'd heard women say that pregnancy can make their skin "glow," but Murph hadn't seen any changes like that. At least not yet. She'd told him about the baby last night over a late dinner. It turned out to be the welcome news he needed to cheer him up after being so stressed over Sally's project encroaching on their area. Though this news had brought a different kind of stress with its added responsibility, it was the kind of stress he didn't mind. The kind related to protecting and providing for his now-growing family. They'd been talking about having kids, but having it happen so soon after that had been a surprise.

As he lay there watching her, he saw she was beginning to wake up. Her eyelids began to flutter, and she then took a big breath.

"Good morning, Mom."

Now her eyes were fully open, and they focused on his as a smile formed on her lips. "Good morning to you, too, Dad."

"Hungry?"

"Happy. But I take it you're hungry."

Murph replied, "With enough coffee, I could hold out until we have brunch over at the *Cove* deck."

"Coffee can wait..." She reached over and pulled him to her.

A LITTLE BEFORE 7:30 a.m...

THE SAME DEPUTY who had responded to the incident at the *Southern Shores* construction site the previous day, Jimmy Kalig, was now on a call about a dead body. The address turned out to be an older but nice double-wide manufactured home on a large, manicured lot that looked like it probably contained a few acres of land. Two pickup trucks were at the house when the deputy pulled up, one under a carport and another parked on the driveway behind it. A man was sitting sideways in the driver's seat of the one parked outside, with his well-worn work boots perched on the running board.

Looking beyond this second truck, Kalig thought he recognized the truck in the carport as the one he'd seen at *Southern Shores* yesterday. As the deputy got out of his cruiser, the man in the pickup also stood up and began to approach him. The guy's skin was darkened from a lifetime of working outside in the sun—all except for his face, which was ashen.

Kalig said, "Are you the one who called?"

The man nodded, took a deep breath and said, "Yeah, I'm Jeff Erneston. We had ah buncha vandalism on our equipment las' night, over at *Southern Shores*, an' then mah boss didn't show up at the job site an' didn't answer his phone. I knew somethin' was real wrong, 'cause he never misses work. I got here an' saw his side door was jimmied, an' nobody answered when I yelled. Found him inside... man, I don't know how anybody could do that ta anybody else..."

"Whoa, slow down a bit. The call said there was a body but didn't mention anything about vandalism. Are you certain he's dead?"

"I kinda figgered some sumbitch takin' a buncha fuel an' oil filters wasn't as important as ah man losin' his life! An' yeah, I'm sure. Ain't nobody kin lose that much blood an' live. They butchered him, man! Go see fer yourself, but I ain't goin' back in there; I don' need ta see that again. Lost mah breakfast over there by th' door. Bill was ah good boss, an' ah tough man. Don't know how somebody coulda done that ta him."

"Okay, you stay here." Kalig turned and approached the door leading inside from the carport, being careful to step around a large puddle of vomit by the door.

Once inside, he found Bill Bendeck tied to a chair, sitting in a pool of blood. Bendeck's throat was slit from one ear to the other, which accounted for most, but not all, of the blood. Each arm had multiple small stab wounds, and one pinky finger had been completely severed and now lay on the floor in the blood pool.

With no doubt in his mind about whether Bendeck was dead or not, Kalig carefully retraced his steps and went outside. He radioed for a crime scene unit and a shift supervisor then began a more in-depth questioning of Erneston.

After the shift supervisor arrived and took charge, and a CSI team, the medical examiner, and another deputy showed up, Kalig went over to the *Southern Shores* job site to investigate Erneston's claim of vandalism, which he thought might be related. Upon arrival, he spotted a maintenance truck pulled up next to the dozer closest to the gate in the fenced equipment corral, and he began questioning the mechanic next to it.

Erneston had been right about the vandalism; every piece of equipment had been stripped of its oil and fuel filters. The fuel lines had also been loosened, letting air into the fuel systems, and now each engine had to be reprimed before it would start.

The mechanic was more frustrated than angry. "I'm only gonna get two ah these goin' today, 'cause that's all th' filters ah got on hand. These ain't filters ya can go get at th' auto parts store on Sundays; I gotta wait an' pick some up from the dealer tomorrah. I only keep th' pair in stock, 'cause they're so damn expensive. Ah order 'em in right afore ah do the oil changes."

Kalig said, "So, how much would you say the damage amounts to?"

"If he didn't do somethin' ta the oil or th' fuel, it weren't much. Ah mean, most of them filters already had a buncha hours on 'em, an' they needed replacin' anyways, so they ain't worth much. Nah, the sumbitch knows engines, I'll give 'im that. Knew how to disable everythin' without costin' a bundle, less'n mah time, ah course. An' now I gotta drain an' change th' oil on all of 'em, just ta make sure it wasn' screwed with. This wasn' kids, it was somebody who knew what he was doin', the sumbitch."

Kalig thought about the incident yesterday and how upset that guy Murphy had been at all the work being done before he could have a shot at getting an injunction in court. Was he upset enough to have sabotaged these machines? *Probably*, he thought to himself. Also, enough to kill the foreman? *Not likely*, he thought. That would require a level of escalation far beyond what he'd seen here yesterday. And then why torture the foreman? How would that further his cause? What did the foreman know that could've been of interest to Murphy? But it was worth going and talking with him. The two men definitely didn't like each other, and Murphy was desperate to get the work stopped long enough to have his day in court. Yeah, it was definitely time for a chat.

Kalig drove across the highway to the restaurant's lot, hoping to get directions to Murphy's house. He parked in an open space next to the dumpsters. Getting out of the vehicle, he was reminded why you never parked next to a seafood restaurant's dumpsters on the weekends when there might be days between garbage pickups.

The stench of rotting seafood was bad enough, but he also caught a slight whiff of something else: diesel fuel. He opened the gates to the walled corral that contained a pair of metal dumpsters. He slid open the side door on one, but he found that wasn't where the odor was coming from. Sliding the access door open on the other one yielded results; inside were over a dozen oil and fuel filter canisters with the brand logos from the earthmover manufacturing company printed on their sides. He thought about climbing in and retrieving all of them but decided that this was a job better suited to the CSI bunch.

Kalig retreated to the parking lot and looked around for any cameras that might cover the dumpster corral but didn't see any. He then went over to the restaurant's entrance. The hostess told him that the Murphys lived in a private compound next door but that he was in luck; they were out on the restaurant's back deck having breakfast. She led him through the restaurant and out on the deck, where he spotted Murphy and an attractive blonde sitting at a table by the railing. Murph looked up as he approached.

"Hello again, Deputy. Have you come in for coffee or brunch? We have the best of both on the Shore."

"No, Mr. Murphy, I need to ask you some questions."

Fortunately, with it being pre-season and rather cool, there weren't any occupied tables near them; most people had chosen to eat inside, so this afforded the trio some privacy.

"Fire away."

Knowing that the vandalism and the murder had happened sometime during the early evening or at some point during the night, he asked, "Can you tell me where you were between the hours of 6:00 p.m. and 6:00 a.m.?"

"Well, sure, I was home smoking bluefish, making fish dip, then having dinner with my beautiful wife here, listening to her tell me about how I'm gonna be a daddy." He grinned as he saw that this last bit of news threw the deputy off a bit. Murph tilted his head slightly as he asked, "Why do you want to know where I was?"

Ignoring the question, Kalig asked, "Uh, Mrs. Murphy, can you verify your husband's whereabouts last night?"

Lindsay hesitated a few seconds before saying, "Sure. I was with him for a while when he was smoking and cleaning the fish, but then I went back to our houseboat when it started getting chilly. I was tired and took a nap until Murph got home when he finished."

"So the smoker isn't at your houseboat?"

Murph answered, "No, it's a communal smoker that a bunch of us use that's over a hundred yards away from our boat. But you didn't answer my question. Why do you want to know my whereabouts?"

"All of the construction equipment across the street was vandalized last night, and I want to know if you were involved."

Murph beamed. "Vandalized? Really? That's great! Couldn't have happened at a better place. And when you say 'vandalized,' what exactly are we talking about?"

Kalig wasn't sure if this news had come as a surprise to Murph, but from her looks, it definitely was to Lindsay. "Fuel and oil filters were removed and stolen, and fuel systems drained. Their mechanic is hoping to get one or two of the machines going today and the rest tomorrow."

"This is AWESOME! I bet Sally Shaw is fit to be tied. This is exactly what I needed to have happen to allow me time to get to court to keep them from wrecking the rest of that property. But I'm sure that between Sally and that asshat foreman, they probably have a list of people that were capable of doing this to them."

"Yes, but I just discovered the stolen filters in your restaurant's dumpster."

Lindsay's face registered surprise and she quickly glanced over at Murph, who still seemed delighted at the outcome. He said, "You mean our dumpsters that are the closest to that job site? The dumpsters that are unlocked and accessible to anyone from our parking lot or who might pass by on the way to their car? Those dumpsters?"

"Yes, the dumpsters owned by the man who was in a physical altercation with the site foreman a few hours before he was murdered."

That obviously surprised and rattled both Murph and Lindsay. "Murdered?" Murph exclaimed.

"Yes, sometime last night. Would you happen to know anything about that?"

"No! Of course not! I don't, er, *didn't* like the guy, but certainly not enough to kill the man. And you think the vandalism has something to do with this?"

"I think it's a strange coincidence if it doesn't."

Lindsay spoke up. "I think if I were going to steal filters off of those machines, I'd probably plan to get those off my truck as soon as possible. And the most obvious and closest dumpsters are ours."

"Why do you think the perpetrator was driving a truck?" Kalig asked her.

"Because I've changed oil filters on our boats. It's a messy, nasty job, and I'd never put them inside of a car—that's just logical."

"And do you have anyone who can verify that you were taking a nap last evening while you waited on your husband?"

"What? No! Do you think I vandalized that equipment? Maybe while Murph was busy killing the foreman? You're never going to make detective at this rate, pal." Lindsay's anger was rising. "We are a couple of job-creating, tax-paying, property-owning, honest business-people, and we don't appreciate these kind of accusations!"

"These are not accusations, just questions that I have to ask, Mrs. Murphy."

"Which sounds a helluva lot more like accusations, Deputy. Asked and answered. And unless you have more accusations to make that are also disguised as questions, then we are done here. We don't know anything about the man's murder, nor any vandalism. Now, please go and let us eat in peace."

Kalig started to say something but then thought better of it. He reached into his pocket and took out a card, which he placed on the table. "If you hear of anything regarding either of these crimes, please give me a call."

He turned and left as Lindsay said, "If I find out who shut down those machines, I'll give them a damn medal."

.   .   .

THE PAIR WERE JUST FINISHING up their breakfast when they spotted Casey coming down the dock, heading for the deck's stairs. He then walked over to their table, and Lindsay motioned to one of their empty chairs. As he sat down, he picked up the deputy's card from the table. "This have anything to do with the missing filters from across the road?"

Lindsay's jaw dropped. "How'd you…"

Murph put a hand on her arm. "Never ask a question that you don't want an answer to. Just remember this phrase, *I have no recollection of that, your honor.* Just be thankful for our visit from the 'filter fairy.'"

Casey grinned. "Don't waste any of this pause in the action. Contact our company attorney today and have her draw up a motion to present to a judge first thing tomorrow morning."

Murph said, "Disappearing filters weren't the only things that he was asking us about. Apparently, that foreman was murdered last night."

The look of shock on Casey's face was genuine, leaving no doubt in either Lindsay's or Murph's minds that he didn't have anything to do with the man's murder. Not that Casey wasn't capable of killing someone; he was, and he had in the past. But all of those people had been threatening Casey or one of his loved ones, and in many cases, they had shot at him first.

Casey's phone rang. He pulled it out of his pocket and grimaced. The caller ID read *Sally*. "Oh, this ought to be good."

8

CHANGE AIN'T EASY

"Good morning, Sally."

"Good morning, my ass, you son of a bitch! You and your butt-kissing buddy Murph aren't going to get away with this!"

Casey grinned. "By 'this,' I guess you mean the vandalism of those machines across the street."

"So, you aren't even going to try denying it?"

"I don't need to try, I'm telling you it wasn't me and Murph. And we didn't murder that foreman, either!"

"Murder? Whaaat?"

"You must've let your subscription to the *ESVA Telegraph* lapse. Someone killed the foreman last night, too."

There was a long pause before Sally replied with a now shaky voice, "I'm carrying my pistol with me."

"That's nice. Are you threatening me, Sally?"

"No, I'm just telling you that I'm prepared to defend myself. Why did you murder the foreman? What did that gain you?"

"I didn't kill the guy; it wouldn't have gained me anything. Be careful about what you say, though, Sally; slander can be very expensive."

She had regained her earlier composure. "Well, if you didn't kill him, who did?"

"How the hell would I know? I didn't even know him! Maybe he had a bitch of an ex-wife with a grudge. You know, like you. But I've spent all the time I'm going to, talking with you about this. Goodbye, Sally."

"I'm not done..."

But Casey hung up before she could finish her sentence. He looked over at his two friends and smiled. "Well, that was fun."

Lindsay said, "You've got a weird definition of 'fun,' Case."

He drew in a deep breath as he closed his eyes and nodded. "I guess." He reopened his eyes as he said, "Sparring with ex-wives should be classified as an Olympic sport." He paused, then said, "Do you know what really chaps my butt? It's the fact that I funded her damn project with our divorce settlement—six million bucks for six months of marriage. I was the biggest idiot on the Eastern Shore, and now I'm paying for it all over again."

Murph said, "Correction, Case. Now we're paying for it." He motioned to all three of them. "But don't beat yourself up too much. You just fell fast and hard and used your wrong head for thinking." He grinned at Casey.

"Casey, you know, when you think about it, you got a bargain," Lindsay said. "You got Dawn in the process and were rid of Sally with that one check. Well, at least you were rid of her until now. We all were. So, now, we'll all deal with her, and hopefully, we can get this thing stopped in court tomorrow."

GREG AND BEN were sitting at the counter having breakfast at the same little place with the great biscuits where the drivers and operators had stopped yesterday morning. Jeff Erneston came in, sat down a couple of seats away, and ordered a biscuit with jelly and a glass of milk. A buddy of his was sitting next to him and began kidding him about his breakfast being a "kid's meal." Neither Greg nor Ben knew either of the men, but Erneston was loud enough that they couldn't help but overhear what he was saying.

Erneston told his friend, "I lost mah first breakfast on account ah I found mah boss's body this mornin'. Somebody tortured and kilt him las' night. Bastard even cut his pinky finger right off, an' slit his throat. Man, I never seen so much blood."

"Why'd you find him, Jeff?"

"Well, we're doin' th' dirt work for that new *Southern Shores* project across th' street from *Mallard Cove*, an' Bill was th' foreman on-site. Somebody stole alla th' filters off th' machines las' night. Normally Bill woulda been th' first one there an' woulda found it, but he never showed. That's when I went ta his house, and found him." He shivered at the memory.

"Damn, man, that's awful! The cops got any idea who did it?"

"I heared two of 'em talkin' about ah fight Bill got inta with one ah the owners ah *Mallard Cove*. Th' deputy had ta break it up. Thought that guy mighta followed Bill home an' finished th' job. But I gotta tell ya; whoever it was is one mean sumbitch. Never seen so much bloo..." At this point, his biscuits arrived, mercifully stopping any further commentary while others around him were eating.

The two brothers glanced at each other, realizing this "Bill" was the guy who had probably taken their thirty grand. Ben was about to say something when Greg shook his head, stopping him and saying, "Finish up; we've got work to do."

Five minutes later, in the privacy of Greg's truck, Ben asked, "Do ya think that was the same guy we saw yesterday?"

"Probably. And if he did take our money, he might have gotten killed for it. The part I don't get is, who else would have known he had it and also knew where he lived?"

"Mebbe he showed it ta somebody onna crew, somebody who knew where he lived."

"That, or somebody followed him home and forced him to tell where the money was. But they'd have had to have known he had it in the first place." Greg thought for a moment. "Did you touch any of the money?"

"Well, yeah, why? Ya know I always count th' rolls, jus' ta keep the Captain honest."

"That means your fingerprints are on the rolls. And if whoever took it gets busted, the cops will likely try to lift fingerprints off all of those rolls."

Ben had a "deer in the headlights" look as he realized what Greg said was true. "What are we gonna do about it?"

"We're not going to worry about it because there isn't anything we *can* do about it. Chances are they'll hide it, just like that foreman must've, or maybe they'll spend it. I doubt anybody would've tortured him just for kicks; they wanted information. There had to be some kind of value there."

"Think they know 'bout us?"

"Not very likely."

THE CAPTAIN FOLLOWED the reverse route of the one he had done yesterday, picking up oysters from a packing house on the back side of the Shore. Then he made what would be his new dope run, past *Casey's Cove* and *Mallard Cove*, then across the bay to his dock on the west side. He offloaded the oysters into one of his small, refrigerated box trucks. He'd just finished that when his best dealer, Jimmy G, pulled in next to the truck.

Jimmy hopped down into the skiff and addressed the Captain. "What up, big guy? You couldn'ta talk ta me onna phone?"

"Ya know, I never talk business on phones. It's a good way ta get caught by John Law. Naw, this hadta get done face ta face."

"Okay, so, whatcha want?"

"It's more like me askin' what you want. I'm increasin' production, an' I wanna know how much more you kin move."

"Ahm movin' all I can right now. I'm gettin' squeezed, an' it's tough jes' holdin' mah territory, yaknowwhatImean? I'd love ta take more product, but that'd take me ta war with Big Lincoln an' your boy

Blade, an' I ain't up fer that. We got a good thing goin', yaknowwhat-Imean? Les jes' keep on keepin' on like we doin'."

The Captain was disappointed because Jimmy G was the dealer he trusted the most, not that he really trusted any of them. Blade probably least of all. While he'd told Greg he would stick to the dealers he already had, that was "Plan A," and it wasn't looking so good right now. But he had a backup, "Plan B," which wasn't going to make Jimmy G happy.

HALF AN HOUR LATER, a big, black Lincoln Navigator pulled into the spot that Jimmy had vacated. Big Lincoln stepped down out of the back passenger door, leaving his driver in the vehicle. Unlike his nickname suggested, this African-American man had only a slight build. His nickname had to do with his choice of ride, though it might also have had to do with his stature on the street.

"Yo, Cap'n. What's up?" He stepped down into the skiff.

"I gotta *big* opportunity fer ya, Lincoln."

The way the Captain had emphasized the word *big* in a play on his name wasn't lost on Big Lincoln, and it irritated him. But rather than make a point of it now, first, he wanted to hear what it was that was on the Captain's mind.

"Up 'til now, I ain't been able ta supply ya with any product, but things jes' changed. I kin offer ya two pounds a week, startin' next week."

Big Lincoln smiled as his eyelids closed to slits. "No, baby, I don't want your couple ah pounds; I'm gonna take all that ya make."

The Captain laughed. "Ah appreciate yer offer, but all I kin give ya is two pounds a week. At least fer now."

"What you gonna do with those other six pounds, now that ya got no place ta go with 'em?"

The Captain shook his head. "No, ya see, those'r already spoken for." He was surprised that Big Lincoln knew exactly how much product he was moving. This wasn't good.

Big Lincoln curled his fingers back against his right palm and pretended to study the fingernails. "Yeah…that might'a been true an hour ago, but let's just say that your boys Jimmy an' Blade ain't gonna be puttin' in no more orders. Their boys are all workin' fo me now."

The Captain cocked his head slightly as he looked at Big Lincoln. The meaning behind the man's words slowly sank in. Apparently, the "war" that Jimmy had mentioned had just happened, though it sounded more like a quick coup. This now made Big Lincoln the biggest meth dealer in Richmond, and the Captain's sole customer.

"Okay…that's great. Less people I hafta deal with." Even though he said this, he felt it was anything but great.

Big Lincoln had a reputation for violence and was obviously very ambitious, which worried the Captain. But he hadn't yet heard what was really going to be his cause for alarm.

"Yeah, less people. But more product." Big Lincoln smiled wickedly.

"Uh-huh. 'Nother two pounds ah week ta produce."

"No, baby. Ya need to double whatcher makin' now. I'm gonna need that much in Richmond, an' startin' in two weeks, I'm gonna need more fo' Fredericksburg, too."

"Uhhh, ah'll have ta check an' see if they kin make that much."

Big Lincoln wasn't expecting this. "Whatta you mean, 'check'?' Jus' tell your cook to make more."

"He ain't exactly my cook. Th' boys are more like independent contractors, ya see."

This was a complication that Big Lincoln hadn't been expecting, but he now recognized it as an opportunity. "Oh, I see all right; you not producin' shit, you nothin' but a damn middleman."

"Not 'xactly. I schedule 'em, an' do all th' pickups an' transportation. They're jus' th' ones who do th' cookin'. Ah take all ah th' risk."

"Okay, then I'm gonna need ta meet yo 'partners.' I don' deal with people I ain't never seen afore."

"They not gonna go fer that, Lincoln. They real careful 'bout privacy an' stuff. Tha's why they got me ta meet wit' everybody else."

"Yeah, like ah said, I'm real careful not to deal with people I ain't never met before. I ain't askin' to meet 'em; I'm tellin' ya ta get it set up."

"I ah...can't reach 'em afore ahm supposed ta pick up th' next load on Friday."

"You cain't cain't call your own cooks?"

"They don't like phones either. Kinda paranoid 'bout security."

The paranoid part Lincoln liked. But not being able to reach them before a pickup was going to have to change. But first things first.

"Okay, then I'm goin' with you on your next pickup."

The Captain shook his head. "Ah don' know 'bout that. They wouldn' like it."

"I bet they wouldn' like not having nowhere ta sell their product even mo' than that."

This was the part the Captain had been afraid would happen. By having only one customer, he'd lost a lot of leverage. He couldn't play one dealer against the other, and he was now more or less at the mercy of Big Lincoln.

Reluctantly, the Captain said, "All right, you kin ride with me. I jes' hope they ain't gonna get mad."

"Yeah, well, that's part of your job as ah middleman, ain't it? You gotta keep yo' boys in line."

After Big Lincoln left, the Captain pulled away from the dock, heading back across the bay to the skiff's slip. Along the way, he pondered the new changes. He realized there were both good and bad sides to things. With only one customer, he lost a lot of leverage. However, one larger customer might also mean since Big Lincoln was so much more powerful, he might have more juice on the street. It might mean he would have an "in" with the cops and know if they were planning on a bust. Maybe be able to "feed" them the names of some of the competition. Plus, having several smaller dealers might also mean one of them would flip on the Captain if they got caught.

Giving up a supplier for a lighter sentence recommendation wasn't all that uncommon, but not at the higher levels. These players had more cash for the best lawyers and an "enforcement crew" that could reach any potential witness or their family. Big Lincoln was already known for his penchant for violence. This made the Captain wonder briefly about the fate of Blade and Jimmy G. But they knew the risks of having somebody like Big Lincoln next to their territory. More than likely, since Big Lincoln had said Jimmy and Blade's boys were now working for him, they were no longer breathing. The Captain grimaced at the thought of what had probably already happened to them.

Now, to get Greg and Ben to agree to this new setup. It had been tough enough to get them to agree to the extra two pounds per week. But now they needed to know this was a matter of life and death. Theirs.

9

TRIALS AND TRIBULATIONS

T wo o'clock Monday afternoon...

"YOUR HONOR, James Robertson, representing Southern Shores Development LLC. As you can see by our brief, the County of Northampton has issued a 'Stop Work' order against my client for work that was being done in accordance with and certified by approvals from the Army Corps of Engineers and the Virginia Department of Environmental Quality. We are well within our rights to proceed. We ask that you order the county to rescind the order."

"Ronald Mosely for Northampton County, Your Honor. The 'Stop Work' order was issued because the county had no advance notice about any work on that site, which was commenced illegally. No permits had been applied for nor issued, and the site was listed as being sensitive wetlands."

Robertson said, "Which is completely covered by our purchase agreement for mitigation credits from our sister company, the Northampton Mitigation Bank. This allows us to change the parcel's designation without notice to the county."

"Your Honor, neither the Board of Supervisors nor the Planning Commission had ever heard of this project until this morning. The developers, Cetta & Shaw, attempted to get the land stripped of vegetation this weekend before the county offices could open and issue the 'Stop Work' notice. If they hadn't run into mechanical issues, they would have accomplished this task before anyone could have done anything to stop the destruction," Mosely stated.

Robertson frowned and said, "Our machinery didn't have 'mechanical issues,' we were sabotaged."

Mosely snorted. "In the middle of trying to put one over on the county."

The judge banged her gavel. "Enough! The 'Stop Work' order remains at least temporarily in effect until I can research this and make a decision. You can expect it on Wednesday."

Robertson said loudly, "Your Honor! With all due respect, my clients can't wait until Wednesday. Every hour those machines can't work costs them thousands of dollars with nothing to show for it."

The judge leaned forward in her chair, "Then I guess it would have been wise for them to meet with the county officials first. Frankly, I'm surprised at Mr. Shaw for not doing that. From what I had heard, it sounded like he and the county were on good terms."

"Uh, my client is Mrs. Shaw, his ex-wife. Mr. Shaw has no interest in this project, financially or otherwise."

"So noted. All right, this hearing is adjourned." The gavel banged.

~

ABOARD THE *LADY DAWN*, Casey, Dawn, Lindsay, and Murph were meeting with their attorney, Jessica Forester.

"I sat in the gallery and haven't submitted an amicus brief to the court yet, nor did I get involved during the proceedings. The last thing we want to do is make it look like it's a fight between two exes. It needs to be the county versus a sneaky developer, period. The judge even commented that he was surprised that you would be involved in this project, but then Cetta & Shaw's attorney cleared that one up that it was Sally and not you.

"The judge didn't sound happy about how the project moved forward, and from talking with the County Attorney, I know they are pissed off over at the county offices. From reading the history of Mitigation Banking, it was originally used for projects in other states. Generally, it was used within a single property to allow for the development of strategically located parts of a parcel while flooding other, less desirable sections. It was only recently that the EPA has bent the rules to allow for credits to be used off-site.

"Here's the part that has the county in a tizzy: these credits could even be used to mitigate a development on the western side of the Chesapeake. If they were used in other areas, Northampton would be losing annual tax revenue from valuable farmland and having to write it down as an almost worthless swamp. This is going to be brought up at the Board of Supervisors meeting tomorrow night. The County Attorney has been asked to draft an ordinance requiring special use permits for any mitigation banks and specifying that the credits be used only in Northampton."

Casey said, "Sounds like they're hot over this."

"Let's just say that neither Shaw nor Cetta are on their 'good list.' And they screwed up by thinking they only needed approvals from the DEQ and the Army Corps of Engineers. While that's actually true right now as far as creating a mitigation bank is concerned, they are still going to need site plan approvals and a long list of permits from the county. I think I can guarantee those will get slow-walked so much they'll look like they are moving in reverse."

Murph asked, "Is there any way they'll be building this year?"

The lawyer smiled. "As pissed off as they are at the county, I'd say the earliest they could even start digging out that marina basin would be three years from now, if then."

Casey smiled at Murph. "Forget what I said about us looking for farmland and pushing for a new law. For once, it seems the local government is already ahead of us."

Murph started laughing.

Lindsay asked, "What are you laughing about?"

"Oh, to be a fly on the wall when Sally finds out she won't be building anything anytime soon. She'll blow a gasket, and since I've been on the receiving end of that when it happens, I can tell you it ain't pretty!"

~

That afternoon at the office of Cetta & Shaw's attorney...

"WEDNESDAY? Are you freaking kidding me? We need to get those dozers moving now! We can't afford to have them sitting there, racking up idle time fees and doing nothing!" Sally was indeed blowing a gasket, just as Murph had predicted.

Robertson said, "There's nothing I can do about it, Mrs. Shaw. In fact, there's no guarantee that the judge will side with us. While the original law dates back to the 1980s, extending it off-site is something relatively new. We're in precedent-setting territory that has yet to be tested in court."

"Damn it! I knew this was too good to be true." Cetta was as mad as Sally, but his anger wasn't all directed at the county; he was also mad *at* Sally. "You were so sure that we only needed those two approvals, and we'd be 'good to go.' Now we're sitting still while the meter is running. Your bank was right; you don't have enough development experience. And now you had me convince my bank that we had everything we needed. If this blows up, I won't be able to get a loan to build an outhouse!"

"What part of 'new' don't you get, Cetta? It's why there's such a high margin of profit, which you jumped at. So, don't blame me because you didn't do your own due diligence!"

"I was relying on you, my partner, who was supposed to have this all figured out!"

"You're the one who's supposed to have all the development experience; you should've known what we needed in order to move ahead!"

"Oh, now it's my fault? I ought to..."

"Mr. Cetta! Mrs. Shaw! Please, stop; this isn't getting us anywhere. Look, there's nothing we can do until after the judge rules. Ordinarily, I'd recommend that you go down to the county and meet with the planning and building people, but since we're already facing off in court, I'd say that ship has already sailed. There's no way they will lift a finger until after we get a ruling. And if it goes against us, you might want to have a plan ready about how to proceed. I'd love to be optimistic, but in this case, I think cautious is more like it."

WEDNESDAY MORNING AT THE COURTHOUSE...

MURPH WAS ALREADY SITTING in the gallery behind the County Attorney when Sally arrived, spotted him, and glared while she sat down on the other side of the aisle.

Then, the judge entered, and everyone in the room stood. She took her seat on the bench.

"Everyone be seated. I can say that what appeared to be a simple case at first turned out to be a bit more complex. In reading the relevant federal code and past court cases regarding this issue, I can see where it might be easy to misconstrue the specifics that are contained within the code. The Northampton Mitigation Bank was well within its rights to move forward after receiving approvals from the Virginia Department of Environmental Quality and the Army Corps of Engineers, and no further permitting was nor is necessary."

"Yes!" Sally couldn't contain her emotions.

The judge hammered with her gavel. "Order in the court! I'm not finished." She glared at Sally.

"I understand that the Board of Supervisors had an emergency meeting last evening and passed a new ordinance prohibiting any mitigation credits that are created within the county from being used in any other county. This would include the Northampton Mitigation Bank."

Sally had already read the new ordinance, so this wasn't news to her. She wasn't happy about it since this cut out some prime customer candidates for her credits, but at least it didn't keep her from using some at Southern Shores.

The judge continued. "In researching this further, I find that these de minimis permit requirements are relevant only to the property where the mitigation credits are created and not to the property where they are ultimately applied. While the use of these credits does automatically negate the wetlands designation when applied, it does not absolve the developer from any additional requirements that are applicable to properties with that same zoning.

"Hence, the reasoning behind the 'Stop Work' notice is deemed to be valid and is ordered to be enforced until such time as the developer of *Southern Shores* is in possession of all of the required permits and documents. This includes but is not limited to approved site plans, an environmental impact study, building plans, an architectural review committee approval, and any building or special use permits that may also be required.

"This hearing is now adjourned." With a final hammering of her gavel, the judge then stood and made her way to her chambers.

Sally was stunned, having watched her financial future implode. She stayed seated in the gallery as the rest of the observers filed out slowly. A reporter started moving her way, but Sally waved the woman away, tersely saying, "No comment."

Finally, when the room was entirely empty except for her, she stood up, making her way out and to her car. She left her phone on silent, not wanting to talk to anyone. She was about to go over to Cetta's office to face him and explain what had happened. She had no illusions about how hard the county would now make it to get all the permits and documents that they'd need. It would undoubtedly take years.

That was time they didn't have since she and Cetta lacked the cash to carry the property for that long. She had used the last of her cash to secure the mitigation bank property and to strip it and flood it. The plan had been to use the development loan proceeds to create *Southern Shores*. But as soon as the bank got wind of this disaster, that loan would surely evaporate.

~

LATE WEDNESDAY AFTERNOON...

CASEY WAS SITTING on the back deck of the *Lady Dawn* when his phone rang. He picked it up on the second ring after seeing the caller's name. "Hello, Glenn." Even though he couldn't see it, Casey knew that Cetta was frowning. At least, that's how he envisioned him right now.

"Hello, Shaw. No doubt you heard what happened this morning in court."

"Yep."

It was really chapping Cetta's ass to make this call, especially since he was almost certain that Casey's group had been behind the sabotage. But he knew that it was time to cut and run as far as the *Southern Shores* property was concerned and time to get as far away from Sally Shaw as possible. He needed a buyer and fast. Someone who not only had the desire to own the property but who had the ability to buy it and who could afford to hold it long enough to obtain all the necessary permits to build on it. Casey's real estate investment group was the most logical candidate.

"I know you had some interest in that property in the past, but the wetlands designation put you off of it."

"Not much has changed."

"I'd say a lot has changed since I now hold enough mitigation credits to eliminate that wetlands designation. Sixty credits, in fact."

"Don't you mean 'we' now hold those? As in, you and my ex-wife? And even with those in hand, it would be a very long time before enough of the dust settles to allow anything to be built over there."

"No, I mean me. Sally and I parted ways this morning."

Casey smiled at the news. "Gee, I'm sorry to hear that, Glenn."

In a sarcastic tone, Cetta said, "I'm sure. Anyway, as part of our breakup agreement, I took title to the property, and I'm willing to make you a good deal." He quoted a price that would be fair if the parcel was indeed mitigated and ready to build.

"I'll pass."

"What? That's a fair price, Shaw!"

"Not in that condition, it isn't, especially since you kicked a hornet's nest over it at the county. I doubt they'd be anxious to see anything built there anytime soon."

"Okay, so what are you willing to pay for it?"

Casey quoted the price that Cetta and Sally originally paid for it.

"What! The credits alone are worth half a dozen times that!"

"Which I'm guessing you probably took in lieu of suing Sally for getting you into this mess. So, that number gets you whole again, and the word on the street is you don't have the spare cash you'll need to hang onto the property long enough to find another buyer. I know your banker, and I guarantee his finger is poised above the 'foreclose' button right now."

"I'm not going to give this property away, Shaw!"

"This is about making you whole, Cetta."

"While you and Murphy make a killing with it in a few years! You two have done enough of that with some of my other properties in the past."

"Glenn, this is about the here and now, not the past. If you want to extricate yourself from this mess, that's the number that'll do it."

"Forget it!" Cetta hung up on Casey.

"Hey, Case!" Murph was walking up on the floating dock next to the yacht.

"C'mon aboard, Murph, I've got great news!"

A minute later, Murph appeared and took a chair next to Casey's. "Better than we got this morning?" When he realized the court's ruling would postpone any development across the street for years, Murph's demeanor had improved a thousand percent.

"Oh, yeah." He recounted his conversation with Cetta.

Murph looked confused. "I thought you said he hung up on you. And why would you want that mess?"

Casey's phone rang. Looking at the ID, he smiled. "Just watch."

He answered the call on speaker, motioning to Murph to stay silent. "Yeah, Glenn."

"I'm not walkin' away from this one with nothin'. Your number and sixty grand; a grand for every credit, and that's giving them away."

Across the table, Murph's eyes popped. He mouthed, *Take it!*

Casey grinned and shook his head. "Pass."

Murph looked like someone had taken his favorite toy away.

Cetta said, "Aw, come on, Casey. I've got to make a little profit on the deal!"

"Glenn, when the bank forecloses on your ass, you sure as hell aren't going to have any profit in that. Then I'll just buy it from them at a discount, and they'll come after you for the difference between that price and the loan amount. Plus, the legal fees and interest. Then there's the damage to your credit by having a foreclosure..."

Cetta was now pleading. "Meet me in the middle, Casey. Thirty grand over the land cost."

"One dollar over the land cost, and you throw those credits in for free."

"Go to hell!"

"See you there." This time, Casey hung up first.

"Casey, have you lost your mind?" Murph was beside himself.

"No, but I'm not going to reward the son of a bitch for trying to put *Mallard Cove* under and using my ex-wife to help him do it. You know better than anyone that when Cetta gets desperate, he does dumb deals. Time for him to make another one."

Casey's phone rang again. He grinned at Murph, "It's showtime! His bank must really be on his ass already." He punched the answer button. "Yeah?"

"Okay, fine. Land cost plus a dollar. But I'll need a contract and a deposit today."

Casey smirked. Yep, he was right about the bank. Undoubtedly, they had also heard the results of the hearing. "I'll email you one in a few minutes; sign it and email a copy, then send me a hard copy via snail mail. And text me your account numbers, and I'll wire that deposit."

"Yeah, yeah, I know how this works."

After Cetta hung up, Murph said, "Great! So, what do you have in mind to build over there?"

Casey got a funny grin as he shook his head slightly. "Nothing. We're going to give it away."

"What? Are you friggin' crazy? I thought we were tryin' to keep from anything being built over there!"

"We are, and we will. And just because we're giving it away doesn't mean we won't be making anything off the deal."

Dawn came through the salon's glass doors with Summer in her arms. She carefully passed her over to Casey, who was now beaming. She said to Murph, "Are you taking notes, Daddy-to-be?"

"Yeah, I am, and I can't wait. But you need Casey to take a mental competency test."

"What?"

"You want to tell her, Case, or should I?"

'Well, since you don't know the whole story, I think I'd better." When he was finished, all four were smiling. The three adults because of a clever plan, and Summer because she had her daddy's attention.

10

RAMP IT UP

Northampton County Offices, Thursday morning...

CASEY AND MURPH were sitting in the office of the Chairman of the Board of Supervisors, Don Rankin. Casey was saying, "I know this property has suddenly become a thorn in your side."

Rankin grunted. "You don't know the half of it."

"Well, we think we've got a solution that takes it out of that category and makes it a huge plus for the county and you plus the rest of the supervisors."

Rankin leaned forward, intrigued. "Go on..."

"Our group is buying that land, along with enough mitigation credits to cover every inch of that acreage."

Rankin frowned. "And you want some favors to push approvals through. I'm not in the favor business."

"Hold on. You might not be in the favor business, but we are. We're taking two-thirds of that parcel, the part that hasn't yet been cleared, applying some of those credits, and then donating it to a conservation land trust. This will guarantee that it will never be built on."

For the first time today, Rankin allowed himself to smile. "And you'll get the tax benefits at full commercial acreage value. Pretty slick, Mr. Shaw. But what about the other third?"

"Call me Casey, please. We are applying those remaining credits to it and donating it to Northampton County, with just a few stipulations attached."

Rankin looked suspicious. "What kind of stipulations?"

"That the county build a public boat ramp, parking lot, and fishing pier on it. We've identified some state and federal grants that would fund almost all of it without using the county's money.

"I'm originally from Palm Beach County in Florida. In my first forty years before I moved here, I saw the population of that county grow by over five hundred percent. Many of those newcomers bought boats, most of them trailer boats. During that time, the county added no new boat ramps and only a minuscule amount of additional trailer parking at those ramps. The result was overcrowded parking areas and people parking up to a mile away from the ramps. It's not a fun way to start a day out on the water.

"I see much the same thing in our future. The current expansion of the Chesapeake Bay Bridge Tunnel will allow double the amount of traffic in the coming years and an influx of new residents. People moving here to enjoy the water will also bring or buy boats, and many of those will be trailer boats as well.

"Right now, when people arrive on the Shore, they see two things: *Mallard Cove* on one side of the road and a swampy, torn-up mess on the other. Wouldn't it be better for them to see a multi-lane boat ramp with ample parking and a beautiful fishing pier? It sends a great message that Northampton embraces the waterfront lifestyle and that you care about the boating community."

Rankin leaned back in his chair, thinking. After a few seconds, he asked, "What's the catch?"

"That *Mallard Cove* can utilize some of the car parking areas for overflow during special events, and also that the county can never use this land for anything else. If they ever decide they no longer need or want it or want to do something else with it, we can buy it back—including any and all improvements—for a dollar."

Rankin leaned forward on the desk and interlaced the fingers of both hands while tapping both pointer fingers together, apparently something that he did when deep in thought. Finally, he looked up and said, "I'll have to run this past the rest of the Supervisors at our regularly scheduled meeting tonight, but I can't imagine any of them turning this down. You're right; it will make a great statement to everyone coming off the CBBT about how much we value our aquatic recreation and how it's a big part of who we are as a community. Thank you both so much for this. Can you come to the meeting and do a formal presentation? I'll get it added to the agenda and make sure that there will be plenty of local media in attendance."

Casey and Murph looked at each other and nodded, grinning. Murph said, "Wouldn't miss it!"

ABOARD HER VINTAGE thirty-two-foot wood sailboat, *Creola*, Sally sat alone in the small cabin, a half-empty bottle of wine in front of her, the second one of these this morning. The past twenty-four hours had been a nightmare. She'd had to give up her claim to half the equity in *Southern Shores* and sixty acres worth of mitigation credits, all just to get that damn Cetta off her ass. She'd retreated to her boat after making the agreement, wanting to lick her wounds and shut out the world.

As much as she now despised Cetta, she hated Casey even more than him. He had to have been the one who sabotaged the dozers and also sicced the county inspectors on their site. He'd wrecked her life yet again. *Southern Shores* was to have been her debut as a developer and a sharp stick in Casey's eye at the same time. He'd have had to look at it every time he came and went out of *Mallard Cove*. That was a big part of why she'd wanted to do the project in the first place. At least now he'd have a partially cleared lot across from him, which had to drive him nuts. So, at least that much good had come from it.

Sally clumsily poured another glass of wine and leaned back in the bench seat. She tried blocking out the memories of Casey and her in this boat and over at *Bayside*, the then-defunct resort property that he'd bought and that had lured him up from Florida. That was before she'd realized what a bastard he really was. Already blocked out of her mind was the fact she'd been the one who had wanted to step out on him with Dawn. Then he'd divorced her and ended up with Dawn, gotten married, and now they'd had a kid together.

No! She wasn't going to allow Casey to wreck her life all over again. She would find a way to make him pay, once and for all. She drained half of her glass in one long gulp.

THAT NIGHT, outside of the Northampton County Offices...

CASEY AND MURPH finished their last impromptu interview on the steps of the building. After they climbed into Casey's SUV, Murph said, "That went over even better than I thought it would!"

Casey nodded as he started the car. "Yeah, I kept waiting to get hammered on us getting the tax write-offs, but that never came. I think most folks were just happy that the county was going to do something good with that property. There weren't a lot of locals who wanted to see more bars and restaurants built there, blocking what's now going to be a great water view that everyone can enjoy."

"Cetta is going to go nuts."

"Screw him. There's nothing he can do about it since we already have equitable title with that signed contract and accepted deposit. It's funny; a year ago, I wanted to buy that property for a small over-flow parking lot. Now, the county is going to do the work for us, and we won't be taxed on it."

~

"Let's go; I want to be sure we get there way before the Captain does. I don't want him to see exactly what canal we came from," Greg told Ben.

"Ah know, ya told me that over'n over. Ah got it."

The two brothers climbed aboard the old steel tugboat, and Greg fired up the engine. Ben untied their mooring lines, and they were off, spinning around in the canal and heading for the Inside Passage. They'd been idling at the meeting place for fifteen minutes before the running lights on the Captain's boat came into view. As he pulled alongside, the brothers realized that he had someone else aboard with him.

"Hey! What the hell gives, Captain? We've told you to always come alone." Greg was angry as well as nervous.

"Yeah, well, boys, things have changed a bit. This is Big Lincoln, an' he kinda took over th' territory mah boys had. But we was able ta make a deal, an' I know you wan' me ta deal with less people, an' tha's what I'm plannin' ta do. Big Lincoln is it. But he's got some great news."

Big Lincoln said, "Nice ta meet ya. Th' good news is I can take these eight pounds twice a week, startin' this Tuesday an' Friday."

"Whoa, whoa, whoa, now hold on. I'm not comfortable having to make double the amount, and growing that fast means a lot more exposure. I don't know you, and for all I know, you might be a narc."

"I ain't no damn cop, idiot. I'm ah man bringin' you business. I'm gonna make y'all rich! You should be thankin' me, not disrespectin' me."

Ben spoke up, "Greg, it'll be cool, man. Les just do our business an' get th' hell outta here."

The Captain replied, "Ben's right. This ain't the time er place ta talk about this with eight pounds ah product an' a ton ah cash out here in th' open. Let's do this deal'n then we kin meet somewhere later an' discuss it."

"Fine, but just you and me. This afternoon at the beach bar at *Mallard Cove*, four o'clock. Now, let's get this over with. Just you and us in the wheelhouse, Captain. Lincoln, you stay here." Greg was still really mad at the Captain. He didn't like how Big Lincoln was dictating things, and the Captain was apparently rolling over for it.

"Don't nobody tell me what ah kin an' can't do, boy," Big Lincoln replied.

The Captain began to plead with Big Lincoln. "Jus' let me handle this, an' ah'll take care ah it."

"Hurry it up." Big Lincoln sounded irritated, but in truth, this was exactly what he had wanted to happen. Once all three were out of sight in the wheelhouse, he took two GPS trackers out of his pockets, switching on each of them. He reached over the side of the tugboat and placed a tracker behind a steel pipe fuel tank vent, out of sight. Then he put the second one up under the deadrise's console. He checked his phone and saw a "thumbs-up" emoji on his text screen. His driver was now able to track both boats on a pad back in the car.

He'd just put his phone away when the Captain reemerged, carrying a canvas bag. He climbed aboard as the tug's engine fired up, and it began pulling away. Big Lincoln told him, "Lemme hold that."

"We kin do our swap over at th' dock, when I drop ya off at yer car."

"What, you don' trust me, Captain?"

"Ah don' know ya yet, Big Lincoln. An' I don' trust too many in this bidness. Tha's how come I ain't been busted."

"Then, git us back ta th' dock, quick. Ah don' wanna be out inna open with product neither."

The Captain advanced the throttle, and the boat climbed up on a plane, the hull shooting spray out each side onto the flat, calm surface of the waterway on this cool spring morning. His mind now drifted to thoughts of all the money he was going to make with all this increase in production. All he had to do was smooth over things with Greg this afternoon. The sun was peeking over the horizon as the Captain and Big Lincoln passed *Casey's Cove*.

Over on *Dorado*, Baloney was enjoying his first cup of coffee up on the flying bridge, as was his normal morning habit. That's when he heard the old two-stroke outboard coming up the Inside Passage. He wondered how much longer that engine would keep running before the owner would be forced to change to a more modern, efficient, environmentally friendly, and much quieter four-stroke motor. Though he kind of liked how the loud motor with its faint smell of burning oil from its mixed gas exhaust reminded him of the boats from his youth. He liked the boat's hull as well since the design hadn't changed much since before Baloney was born. *No need to mess with success,* he thought, as the boat disappeared around the bend, making the turn toward Fisherman Inlet Bridge. He went back to enjoying his quiet, peaceful view of the new day.

A LITTLE OVER *an hour after sunrise...*

CASEY SAT on *Lady Dawn*'s back deck, having coffee and reading the latest online edition of the *ESVA Telegraph*. There was a great article about their investment group taking over the *Southern Shores* site and gifting it to the county. Alongside the article was a nice picture of him and Murph giving their presentation to the Board of Supervisors.

"Good morning, Daddy." Dawn had walked out with Summer, once again putting her in Casey's arms. Even with the pacifier in her mouth, he could see his daughter was smiling at him. "How'd it go last night?" Dawn had been asleep when Casey had gotten home. Nighttime feedings had drastically rearranged her sleep schedule.

Casey handed her his notebook, which was open to the story. She read it and looked at the photo. "Nice! Great that they said we took it over from Cetta & Shaw and that we were not related to the Shaw part of that company. This really ought to burn Sally's ass!"

Casey nodded. "A nice side benefit. I just wish she'd get over herself and leave us alone."

Dawn snorted. "And that won't be happening, Case."

"No, I suppose not. But a guy can dream, can't he?" He grinned widely, not at that thought but because of Summer smiling up at him. He rocked her slightly from side to side. He couldn't imagine life getting any better than it was right now.

With the threat of competition from *Southern Shores* now gone, Murph and Lindsay could relax about their future income from *Mallard Cove*. Another huge plus was that Casey wouldn't have to look at that sign with Sally's and Cetta's names on it anymore.

Much to Murph's surprise and delight, Casey had used his front bumper guard to push the sign over on their way home last night. Soon, it would be replaced by an even bigger sign with an artist's rendering showing the proposed boat ramp and fishing pier. Included at the bottom would be a list of the grants as well as private foundations that were donating funds. But in larger letters above all of them was going to be the name of their group, a nice reminder to all that they did give back to their community.

As Casey looked at his little daughter's smiling face, he daydreamed about when she would be old enough for him to teach her how to fish and run boats. The next decade or two were going to be great ones.

ON THE WAY back to their canal, Greg had been fuming. "I can't believe he would bring someone else along with him! He knows that's been our strictest rule: nobody else knows about us. Now look where we are. Some big dealer not only knows what we look like, he's dictating terms to us!"

Ben had been counting the rolls of cash, but now he looked up. "Yeah, but thinka how much more money we gonna make."

"Yeah, little brother, but how do you spend it from prison? Or worse, if you're taking that long 'dirt nap'! We don't know this Lincoln guy, and it sounds like he's already taking over Richmond. One thing I know about distributors is that they don't just give up their territories without a fight. There's probably a trail of bodies over there."

"Mebbe so. But that ain't our part ah the business; tha's why we got th' Captain. Let him worry 'bout that."

"He better be worrying about ME, and our meeting later today. He's got a lot to answer for."

11

ADOLPH, ELMO, OR DARTH

S ally got up around noon with a hangover that would have killed a mule. She opened her tablet to check the local news. Her head felt like it exploded when she saw the top story and the accompanying photo. Casey and Murph had not only ruined her, but they'd also pulled off a public relations coup with *her* property, and *her* mitigation credits. Feeling completely humiliated, she screamed, and sat down, sobbing. Finally, she pulled herself together enough to go back to her bunk and crawl under the covers.

BIG LINCOLN and his driver waited patiently in the *Mallard Cove Restaurant* parking lot for Greg and the Captain to show. They planned to tail Greg when he left and find out where he lived. Soon, it would be time to remove the middleman and negotiate a new deal directly with the cook. This would happen after a few more loads when he got used to handling the additional volume. To do that, Big Lincoln would first need to know where the man stayed.

Fortunately, he didn't have long to wait, as both parties arrived on time. He pointed Greg out to his driver from the anonymity of their limo-tinted windows. The driver had already seen the Captain back at the dock, so he knew him on sight. But Lincoln needed him to be able to recognize both men if he ever got sent to surveil one or both in the future. For now, they would wait and watch until the two disappeared into the beach bar. While the men walked together; their body language was tense, anticipating the upcoming conflict.

One of the GPS transmitters had revealed the location of the small workboat marina where the skiff was docked, but not the Captain's home. The location of the brothers' tugboat had already been pinpointed, also by Lincoln's hidden transmitter. Now his driver slipped over next to both men's trucks, attaching hidden transmitters to each. Big Lincoln checked the iPad screen and saw they had become active. He told his driver, "Let's bounce to th' far end ah the lot. I don' want ta take a chance on 'em spottin' us. We got them now, wit' th' bugs in place."

AT A FAR CORNER table in the uncrowded bar and grill, the two men ordered beers. After they were delivered, Greg started the conversation, keeping his voice low. "What the hell were you thinking, bringing that Lincoln guy with you this morning? Wasn't I clear about never doing anything like that?"

"Yeah, but this was an emergency."

"Oh, really? Who died?"

"I think maybe mah two best buyers. Neither one of 'em are answerin' their phones. And ya heard Big Lincoln, now he's runnin' their dealers an' corner boys. An' that can only mean one thin': their bosses ain't aroun' no more."

"That's no excuse for bringing him along on the pickup. You think that he may have murdered your buyers? Are you friggin' kidding me?" Greg was fuming.

"Yeah, well, iffin I didn't bring him, we wouldna had any pickup. He won't deal wit' anybody he don' know."

"Exactly my point; you're supposed to be that guy he knows! I don't want to deal with him. What the hell do you think you get paid for?"

"My markup is so ah take care ah th' buyers, an' ta get it all sold, which is what ah been doin'. But I got nobody else ta sell ta that can take that kinda weight every week. An' ya heard th' man; he wants ta *double* that! He's gonna expand, an' he needs more product. Our product!"

"Whose product? I don't see your ass sweatin' over a cook that can explode if you aren't careful! Plus, it's getting tougher to get the precursors in the quantities we need without drawing attention to ourselves."

"Th' pre *whut*?"

"Precursors. The chemical ingredients."

"Why didn'cha jus' say so?"

"Whatever. But you knew I wanted to stay small. Getting bigger attracts more attention, which is what I don't want any part of."

"It was go wit' him, or fold up."

"I don't like the guy," Greg said.

"Ah ain't crazy 'bout him neither, but what other choice we got?"

"Shutting down might have been the better option."

"Don' even kid 'bout that! We got a good thin' goin', an' let's keep it that way."

"I wasn't kidding. You know that old saying: 'Pigs get fat, but hogs get slaughtered.' I was reminding Ben this morning that we can't spend that extra cash if we're in prison. That, or if we're dead. I do not trust that guy Lincoln."

"Ah, he ain't that bad, at least he ain't the worst this bidness got ta offer."

"Not that bad...even though he may have murdered your buyers. Yeah, well, I don't want to see him again. From now on, it's just you that I'm dealing with, or I'll shut it down."

"Okay, okay! Just me; ah got it."

"And for springing him on me this morning, you can pick up the tab for my beer."

"Hell, Greg, a few more months like this'n an' I'll buy th' whole damn brewery!"

"Here he comes, boss." From their far vantage point, Big Lincoln's driver had spotted Greg sauntering toward his truck.

Big Lincoln checked his watch. Five minutes had elapsed since Greg had gone in with the Captain. His pace suggested he hadn't left in a huff, but the short amount of time he'd been in there suggested a direct conversation, with no lingering over lunch. This morning he had been direct and to the point, too. He liked that about Greg, though that was about all he liked about him. That, and his product, of course, which was the best and strongest on the street.

"Okay, les give him two minutes, an' we'll folla him. I got him on th' pad."

"Got it."

Finally, a little after four in the afternoon, Sally reemerged from under the covers. Empty wine bottles littered the tiny galley in the boat, and there were no new "soldiers" aboard to replace the dead ones. But there was about a half-inch worth of whiskey in a bottle under the sink. She needed something to help with the shakes that she had developed over the last two days.

The glass she poured the last of the whiskey into was empty in a few gulps, and then she was left with no choice but to go out to the store for replacements. She was barely in any condition to drive, but there weren't any personal shopping services near where she lived, so, she got into her Jeep. She drove first to the McDonald's drive-thru in Cape Charles, ordering a Quarter Pounder meal with a Coke.

Normally, this was her go-to hangover cure, but since this would be the first solid thing she'd eaten in almost two days, she decided to pull into the corner of the parking lot, taking her time and eating it slowly. This was the smartest choice she'd made all day. Twice she had to fight to keep the burger from coming back up, but it was worth the struggle as it helped to calm her shaky hands. That is, at least it calmed and sobered her up enough to go into the liquor store about a mile from there.

Arriving at the liquor store, she grabbed a cart, then proceeded to fill it with two cases of wine, and a couple of bottles of whiskey. The clerk's assistant put it all into two cardboard boxes, then took it out on a hand truck to Sally's Jeep, loading it into the back. Sally was about to close the rear hatch when she spotted Murph pulling in two spaces away. As he got out of his truck, she began screaming at him.

"You son of a bitch! You and your pal ruined me! Then you used the very credits I created to jack up the value so you could get a bigger write-off!"

"Hey, slow your roll there, sweety! If we hadn't bought that property when we did, the bank would have foreclosed on you and Cetta. We'd have still ended up with the property anyway but at a much lower price. Then the bank would have come after you two for the difference, and you'd have a foreclosure on your lending record in addition to that. You should thank us for saving your ass!"

"Thank you? You want me to thank you? Are you kidding me? Here's your thank you, asshat!" She grabbed one of her bottles of whiskey and hurled it at Murph, who ducked. The bottle sailed past him and smashed on his side window, which somehow managed not to break as well. Broken glass and whiskey cascaded down the door. "I'll get you; I'll get all of you!"

The liquor store manager came out and yelled to Murph, asking if he needed the cops. He shook his head. Upon hearing the manager, Sally slammed the back hatch, then quickly climbed into her Jeep and drove off. Now she really needed another drink.

"She was completely unhinged! I mean, we've all seen Sally when she goes off, but you've never seen her like this before!" Murph was in the salon of *Lady Dawn*, telling Casey, Dawn, and Lindsay what had happened at the liquor store.

Dawn said, "I was hoping that after her project failed across the street, we'd have seen the last of her."

Murph snorted. "Wishful thinking. You know what they say, evil never dies, and in this case, it won't go away. That witch is pure evil."

"Fortunately, the evil part didn't help her aim, babe. I'm glad she missed you." Lindsay was sitting next to Dawn, who was holding a sleeping Summer.

Casey was sitting by himself in a chair, quietly listening to the others. He looked sad; silently blaming himself for having originally brought Sally into the group, and thinking about how the misery she'd heaped on them was all his fault. Dawn saw this and knew exactly where his head was.

"She's a miserable person, Casey. You can't blame yourself for that. She's the one who jumped headfirst into that project without having any idea about what she was doing. She only knew that it would hurt you. Hurt all of us. Like Murph said, she's evil."

Dawn passed Summer to Lindsay, who adored her. Then Dawn went over behind Casey's chair, bent down, and hugged him. "This is not your fault. Sally is never satisfied; she always wants something more, and she loves trying to make you miserable."

Casey nodded. "You're right. Not only does she want more of everything, but she also wants to hurt all of us while doing so if she can. Though she used to try doing that with words, not booze bottles. It sounds like she's getting worse."

"And more dangerous, Case," Murph said. "I'm telling you, you need to be careful when you're out anywhere with Summer. Both of you need to be aware of your surroundings, even more than usual."

"Murph is right, dear. When we start taking Summer with us on errands away from *Casey's Cove*, we'll need to be extra vigilant." Dawn looked worried. It hadn't occurred to her before that Sally might get violent around her baby. But now she wasn't discounting the idea that she might also try to hurt Summer. She felt a sudden chill and hugged Casey even tighter.

Casey replied, "Trust me, I'll be watching for her."

HALF AN HOUR LATER, Murph motioned to Casey for him to follow as he went out the salon's side door. The conversation between Lindsay and Dawn had switched to babies and raising children in general. While Murph and Casey were interested in kids, they were more into the idea of playing with them when they got older. Teaching them how to fish, swim, and dive was more in their mindset, even though Summer wasn't even crawling yet, and Murph and Lindsay's child was only the size of his thumb so far.

"Hey, Case, you want to go to *C2* and grab a beer? It's not exactly fair for us to drink in front of Lindsay."

"Sounds like a plan. Dawn can have a glass of wine, but it has to be three to four hours before she breastfeeds Summer again. And I don't think they'll miss us, since they're so deep into their kiddo conversation." He led Murph down the gangway and onto the dock as they walked to *C2*.

"Here's the thing: I'm not into learning every little thing about breastfeeding and diapers, Case."

Casey laughed. "You may not be equipped for the feeding part, at least until she switches to formula and baby food. But there are a few tricks to changing diapers."

"Wait, you mean YOU change diapers?"

"Well, yeah. I mean, that's the part I am equipped to do!" He held out his hands. "Look Murph, opposable thumbs!"

"Very funny. Now I guess Lindsay will expect me to change diapers, too."

"Why the hell not?" Casey was surprised at Murph. "Won't you want to lend a hand with her or him?"

"And that's another thing, Case. What if we have a girl? I wouldn't know what to do with a daughter."

"You think that I did? It'll come to you. The first time Summer looked up at me and smiled, my heart melted. I knew I wanted to hold her, but then all of a sudden I realized I was rocking her in my arms, very gently. It was instinctive. Oh, and by the way, if you guys have a son, you've got to move. Far, far away from here and my daughter!" He chuckled.

"Yeah, right. I hope it is a he, just to watch you squirm when they go out fishing together by themselves when they're teenagers!"

"I'm going to hire security guards to keep an eye on Murph, Junior."

Murph got a funny, faraway look on his face.

"What is it, Murph?"

"Murph, Junior. I hadn't even thought about names yet. Wow. I guess that it could be Michael Murphy, Junior, couldn't it?"

"Better than Adolph, Elmo, or Darth." Casey chuckled, amused at where Murph's mind was wandering. "But only slightly."

"Wow. A son. That would be so cool."

"And you're just now considering that this may be a possibility?" They had reached the mini-fridge at *C2*; Casey reached in and then handed Murph a beer.

"Honestly, I'm just getting over the shock of finding out we're pregnant. Plus, with everything else that has been going on around here…"

"Understandable. I'm hoping that things are going to settle down a bit now that we've headed off the competition across the road."

They sat in a pair of lounges, looking out over the basin of *Casey's Cove*. Murph nodded as he said, "We're just lucky that Cetta got so jammed up at the bank, and we could derail that project. It could have just as easily been one of those sharks from Virginia Beach that bought the property and built that same complex those two had in mind."

Casey gave Murph a sly smile. "Well, luck might've had a little bit to do with it."

"What else could it have been?"

"You heard me tell Cetta that I knew his banker."

"Wait…you mean…"

"He and I are friends, and I pointed out what a nightmare this was about to become for the bank. I merely suggested that there might be a much better alternative."

Murph whistled. "You set Cetta up!"

"Somebody needed to. You didn't want to keep him as a neighbor, right?" Casey's smile was now as wide as it could've been.

"Remind me never to play poker with you, Case."

"Stick with me. We've got a lot of things to do ahead of us."

"Trust me; I'm not going anywhere."

"Unless you have a son. Then you're evicted."

12

FISH ON!

On Tuesday, the Captain met the boys at the new spot, making the transfer. Greg was happy to see that the Captain had come alone this time. He had been prepared to shut down the operation if Big Lincoln had been in the boat again.

Making as much product as Big Lincoln wanted was taking a toll on Greg. It wasn't as simple as increasing the quantity of each batch, it meant adding batches. The liquid mixture that eventually turned into crystals became more and more unstable in larger quantities. Greg knew that if it began reacting or was exposed to a spark, the whole barge would blow, and there would be no escaping the blast's concussion.

He thought back to his conversations with Jeff Emery about how he had built the business, increasing the quantities gradually. Of course, that had been back in the trailer days, with smaller and more inferior equipment. It was only because Greg had upgraded all that and created the new space that he was able to handle such a large increase in production. Even so, it was taking up so much more of his time. The money was nice, but just as it had been for Jeff before him, it had become a trap for Greg. What good was having so much cash that you couldn't spend it all, anyway? The new production schedule had even taken away a large chunk of what had been his leisure time.

Greg wasn't yet ready to tell Ben, but he had begun planning an exit strategy. They had fallen into this business because they were in a bind over taxes, but they could phony up some labor receipts so that was no longer an issue; they could "wash" and then use enough of the pile of accumulated cash for their monthly expenses plus the annual taxes.

Like that movie character, Forrest Gump once said, "Mama said there's only so much fortune a man really needs, and the rest is just for showing off." Only, the brothers couldn't do any showing off. Attracting attention was a great way to get busted. No, Greg had decided that once they had enough money stashed, they would invent a fictional investor that was going to "loan" the brothers enough cash to buy the equipment they'd been lacking to make their marine construction business profitable again. Then, they'd no longer be under the thumb of guys like Big Lincoln, and the money they made would be clean and spendable.

But for now, Greg was keeping this plan to himself. He was expecting a lot of pushback from his little brother, who liked not having to work as hard for a lot more money than he'd ever made before. Of course, Ben wasn't the one having to do all the cooking; he didn't know how. Greg wanted to keep it that way. He didn't want him to be anywhere near that part of the operation.

Back at the barge, Greg already had a head start on making Friday's order. As usual, Ben was keeping a lookout while his brother was belowdecks. Greg was letting his mind wander a bit, daydreaming of the last batch he'd ever make. He was close to the amount of money it would take to fulfill his plans, but he wanted just a little bit more, so they had a hedge against anything that might go wrong. He thought again about that saying, "Pigs get fat, hogs get slaughtered." He was bound and determined not to become a hog.

LATE IN THE day at *C2*, Sandy had brought along two six-packs to put into the outdoor kitchen's fridge. As much as he loved drinking everyone else's beer, now and then he was hit with a bout of remorse, then he would replenish the supply a bit. As he was bent over to load the bottles, he heard, "Hey, ya hack! Make yourself useful an' pull me out a cold one while yer down there."

Instead, he brought out two, handing one to Baloney. "Here you go, Gilligan!"

"How many times do I gotta tell ya not ta call me...oh, never mind. Cheers!" He held his bottle up and Sandy clinked his against it. The two then sat in a pair of cushioned patio chairs.

After a long sip, Sandy asked, "What are you hearing about any fish schools arriving? I saw online that the temperature at the sea buoy is up over seventy now."

"One ah th' net boats said they saw ah buncha glass minnows offa Carolla, an' they were gettin' hit by blues an' somethin' else. He thought it might be mackerel."

"Now we're talking! That bluefish dip was good, but it needed the mackerel. Mahi, too, but we'll be another month or so before they're here. Hey, maybe I'll take *Betsy* down the coast tomorrow morning and see if I can't run into those blues and macks. You want to come along with me?" *Betsy* was Sandy's thirty-seven-foot center console outboard that had been willed to him by his late girlfriend, world-class fisherwoman Betsy Riggins. He had named the boat in her memory.

"Are ya thinkin' mebbe ya can talk Case or Murph inta makin' more Chesapeake Crack dip? It'd be better, made wit' both kindsa fish."

"You're reading my mind, Gill...er...Baloney."

"Wha...? I finally got ya trained now?"

"Nope. Just saving the Gilligan jab for when I've got a larger audience."

Baloney's unlit cigar started acting like a maestro's baton, bouncing around in his mouth. "Hack."

Sandy grinned, then looked past Baloney and said, "Speak of the devils!"

Murph and Casey were talking as they rounded the corner of the boat shed, but they stopped upon hearing Sandy's comment.

"What did we do now? Whatever it is, we're not guilty," Murph said.

Baloney replied, "Hah! Blamin' you fer everythin' is usually a good bet. But in this case, ahm runnin' down th' coast ta try'n get on some macks an' bluefish inna mornin'."

"Oh, hey, if you get enough, we can smoke up a new batch of Crack," Casey offered.

Sandy grinned, "Hey Gilligan, why didn't we think of that?"

Murph reached into the fridge for beers for him and Casey. "What the heck? These are warm!"

"Reach aroun' inna back for th' cold ones. We thought we'd replace some," Baloney said.

Sandy put on a shocked face. "What is this 'we' and 'I' you keep saying when it was 'me' and 'my'? You're worse than a plagiarist!"

"It don't matter, ah'll share some ah th' credit with ya."

"I'll head Gilligan off at the pass and invite you boys to make the run with us if you'd like. We're taking *Betsy*."

Casey nodded, "I love this time of year! Yeah, I'm up for it. Murph, how about you?"

"I'll check with Lindsay, but yep, I'd like to go."

"Since when do ya ever check wit' Lindsay ta get permission about goin' fishin'?" Baloney was surprised.

"Since his better half is now his one-and-a-half," Casey said.

"Oh, yeah, I forgotaboudit. I guess that'd be a good thing ta do then."

Murph looked at Baloney, "Gee, ya think?"

Baloney nodded. "She's a great gal, an' ya better treat her like ah queen fer puttin' up with yer butt, Murph. An' now she's gonna have a lil' Murph or ah Murphette. Summer's gonna have a playmate, that's great!"

The reference to the fact that it might turn out to be a boy threw Casey again. He changed the subject. "What time tomorrow, fellas?"

Sandy said, "Six o'clock. That'll give us enough sunlight to be able to see any fish working the minnow schools. Though the birds will probably be there, too. I'll have us iced down, rods all rigged and ready."

~

WEDNESDAY MORNING...

SUNRISE WAS GETTING EARLIER and earlier every week as the Northern Hemisphere moved toward summer, and they did indeed have plenty of light to work with. As they headed south across the mouth of the Chesapeake, they passed a bait boat headed in the same direction. Another good sign that there might be mackerel ahead. Hook-caught mackerel were in high demand by some tuna fishermen as well as marlin anglers.

When they reached the Virginia Beach side of the bay's mouth, they kept about a quarter mile off the beach, far enough out to avoid any swimmers, but close enough not to miss seeing schooling fish. That's when Baloney recognized the old deadrise skiff with the two-stroke engine just ahead of them and also running south. A couple of plastic sixty-gallon drums with the tops cut off were now in its stern. Sandy stayed about a hundred feet off his beam as they passed. The man running the boat didn't bother either looking over or waving. Not the friendliest type.

Halfway between Rudee Inlet and the North Carolina state line, they spotted birds diving on a brown mass a little more than fifty yards off the beach. Fortunately, the ocean was almost flat, with little one-foot rollers, and not much of a breeze yet, though it was forecast to pick up as the day wore on. It was easy to get close to the school without having to worry about getting caught in any surf.

They were the first on the fish, without any competition, at least for the moment. Sandy had slowed to idle speed and now took both engines out of gear, allowing the boat to finally stop, ten yards out from where he believed the glass minnow school to be. Also called silversides, they were so named because their bodies were partially translucent, and partially silver mirrored. They were covered in a mixture of tiny scales and slime that could quickly cover most surfaces they came into contact with.

Within a minute of their arrival, they saw some fish breaking the surface over the top of the school, and these appeared to be bluefish. There were also some fast-moving silver streaks below the surface which looked to be macks. Both species had mouths filled with sharp teeth, and soon there were numerous pieces of minnows floating on the surface. These leftovers from the feeding frenzy that was now in progress also left small pockets of iridescent scales in the water. These bits and pieces of fish flesh were quickly grabbed and devoured like a free breakfast by numerous laughing gulls. Their voices sounded almost like they were complaining as they fought each other in midair over the scraps.

The four men started using their spinning rods, casting silver Clarke spoons out past the school, reeling them in faster as they got near the school. Ahead of each spoon was a piece of leader wire about a foot long, a necessary addition to combat all those teeth.

"Fish on," Murph yelled, as his rod displayed a healthy bend.

"Make that two," Sandy said, joining the fight. He was able to bring his fish to the side of the boat first, a healthy foot-and-a-half-long mackerel.

Murph had his fish aboard a minute later, a nice-sized schoolie bluefish, perfect for smoking. Then, all four men cast again, with Baloney getting the longest distance of all, overshooting the school by several yards, but getting immediately hooked up with a much larger bluefish. He tried reeling it in, only to have the fish strip off more line instead. Using the light spinning tackle they'd brought was proving to be quite a challenge, even though it was on the stronger end of the light tackle spectrum.

Out of the corner of his eye, Baloney spotted the old deadrise approaching on the far side of the school. Horrified, he realized that the boat wasn't going to slow down in time. It was headed right for his line, which the bluefish had brought up next to the surface. Baloney frantically tried waving the boat away, then started cursing as well as waving. The driver didn't seem to notice him, as he maintained his course.

"Ya moron! Can'tcha see I got ah line out here!"

Again, Baloney's warning went unheeded, as the engine ran over his line. Furious, instead of tightening down on the drag and breaking it off, Baloney opened the drag, watching as well over two hundred yards of braided monofilament began peeling off the spool and wrapping itself around the guy's prop.

"Gilligan! That's my braided line!" Sandy had supplied the morning's tackle along with his boat.

"Yea, well, ya needed ta change line anyway, an' this stuff is perfect for cuttin' through lower unit drive shaft seals!"

"And it's expensive! You could've broken it off and only lost a yard or two, but now I'll have to replace all of it!"

Baloney smiled. "Yeah, but you'll be gettin' off ah lot easier than that bozo, who's gonna have ta replace his lower seal an' all th' gear oil that'll be contaminated with salt water." His grin got wider as the line finally snapped after reaching the knotted end at the bottom of the spool.

Baloney was right about the line doing a number on the guy's driveshaft seal. There was a small space between the prop hub and the lower unit itself. Whenever someone ran over a fishing line, invariably a lot of it ended up worming through this space and winding up around the shaft itself. This brought it into contact with the rubber seal Baloney was talking about. The line then worked its way up to and underneath this critical seal, which allowed saltwater intrusion into the gear oil.

Left alone, this oil and seawater mixture eventually corroded the gears and the casing, ruining the lower unit. This was exactly what Baloney wanted to happen, in retaliation for the guy cutting off his fish. And he had not only screwed up Baloney's fishing, he'd come in fast and close enough to the school to spook the two predator species. They had now sounded, shutting off "the bite," at least for the moment.

Sandy still had a fish on, a nice mackerel, which he landed a minute later. He then took the controls again and then moved up opposite the skiff and yelled, "Hey! Next time how about coming up nice and slow so you don't scare the fish and kill the bite. And while you're at it, try to avoid running over the line of someone who is fighting a fish!"

The Captain looked over at the big center console and the guy who was yelling at him. "What, ya think ya own the ocean 'cause ya got that big rig? Bugger off, ya asshat!"

"Hey, pal, that was my fish ya cut off. An' ya owe me for a whole spool ah braided mono, ya jerk! Next time I'll jump on there wit' ya, an' teach ya some manners!"

The Captain flipped off Baloney as he began idling faster while letting out his line for trolling.

Casey said, "No sense getting upset, guys. Looks like you've got somebody there who's a few brain cells short of an imbecile. Hey, look! They're back up." He pointed to the north of their position where the minnow school was moving, and the predators were now back to feeding, breaking the surface of the water.

Sandy spun around, his bow now pointed in the same direction as the school was moving. He moved up alongside slowly and quietly. Baloney had grabbed one of the spare rods, and he quickly cast into the boiling mass of fish, rewarded by a quick hookup. All three of his companions also began casting, with only Murph retrieving this first cast without a bite. On his second cast, he hooked up.

A couple of hours later, the bite was over for the morning. Several laughing gulls floated lazily in the spot where they got their last bites of fish. A couple took flight, hoping to discover a new spot with more wounded fish, but that wasn't going to be until the next tide, a few hours from now.

Sandy said, "Well boys, we've got a pile of fish to clean. Ready to head back?"

"Let's roll," Murph answered, as Sandy shoved the throttles forward. All four settled in for the forty-minute ride back to the *Cove*. Since it was the middle of the week and there wasn't much traffic, it was a great, smooth ride. This, despite the breeze having picked up, and the waves now running around three feet. While they had a boat and tackle to wash, and fish to smoke, the ride itself was worth all the effort.

BACK SOUTH OF RUDEE INLET, the Captain finally gave up on the bite and decided to run home. As he advanced his throttle up to cruising speed, he heard an unfamiliar sound from the engine, and the boat wasn't moving as it should've. He stopped, shut the engine off, and raised it. That's when he saw the wad of fishing line wrapped around his prop. He realized that it had something to do with that jerk in the big center console named *Betsy*.

Taking his fillet knife back with him, he leaned over the transom and started cutting away the line. Cursing that guy, he made a mental note to keep an eye out for that boat so he could give him a piece of his mind when he saw it again.

Finally, after cutting and removing all the visible braided monofilament, he restarted his engine and headed home again. This time the boat got up on a plane quickly, and the prop was no longer cavitating, which was what had been making that earlier noise back by the engine. Unfortunately, the Captain wasn't aware that the remaining line was now tearing up his lower unit's oil seal. Some lessons had to be learned the hard way.

13

ON NOTICE

Back at *Casey's Cove*, Baloney "supervised" while Murph and Sandy washed down the boat and tackle, and Casey began cleaning the fish. Except that his "supervision" was limited to him sitting in a chair, drinking a beer, and pointing out any spots they missed with soap or bits of meat that got left on a fish carcass.

"You know, you could get your ass down here and start using a chamois to dry the parts we're through with, Gilligan," Sandy said.

"Yeah. No, I don't wanna risk mah beer leavin' a sweat ring on your pretty boat. Youse guys are doin' great, so keep it up."

Casey shook his head and chuckled. Typical Baloney. Then he saw Lindsay and Dawn rounding the corner of the boathouse. Lindsay was carrying a large stainless-steel bowl filled with mustard sauce, while Dawn had Summer in an infant carrier.

"Hey, hey! It's my daughter's first time here at C2. Hello, Summer!"

Dawn said, "She's out cold. She was a very busy baby while you were gone. Breakfast, burps, nap, diaper changes, lunch, burps, nap, another diaper change, and now her first outing. An exhausting day for a little one."

"Yes, but doesn't this feel like it's why we built this place? It's finally going to be used like it's intended?" Casey smiled at his daughter.

"Uh, Case, she's not quite ready to swim yet," Dawn said and laughed.

"I'm not talking about swimming, I'm talking about having not just friends but family around us, too. There's just one thing missing, and I'm going to start researching it after I'm finished here."

"I hate to ask..."

"A swing set, of course! We'll have to pick the right one that can grow with her and little Murphette," Casey said.

"Murph, Junior," Murph said loudly from over on *Betsy*.

Lindsay looked at the two men like they'd lost their minds. "She's only a month old, guys! Don't you think she needs to be walking first?"

"Oh, that reminds me, I need to get a pool kiddie fence installed right away. You can never be too careful," Casey added.

Lindsay and Dawn looked at each other, shaking their heads. Dawn said, "I think you have plenty of time, Casey."

"It's never too early, Dawn, and we don't want to forget to do it. Oh, and we need gates on the stairs on the boat and drawer, door, plus cabinet safety latches. I'll talk with Captain Frank about the best ones to buy."

WHILE THE SAFETY conversation was going on at *C2*, an entirely different conversation was occurring in a sporting goods store in Virginia Beach.

"This model is the most powerful one allowed for civilians, as well as the longest range on the market. Quick change magazines and a great green daylight laser sight."

"Any recoil with it?"

"None to speak of. Another of the big advantages."

"I'll take it and a pair of spare magazines."

At the register, the salesman rang up her purchase, and Sally

Shaw handed him her credit card. She smiled as she pictured how she would use this.

The salesman handed back her card and the bag with her purchase. "Here we go. Have a great rest of your day, and happy hunting."

"Thanks, it will be, on both counts."

~

THURSDAY AFTERNOON...

GREG WALKED across the lot from the barge over to the house. He went inside and then grabbed a beer out of the refrigerator. He found Ben watching an old movie on cable in the living room, and he collapsed onto the sofa.

Ben asked, "Tired?"

"Tired of the whole damn thing. I don't like how the Captain seems to have bent over for Big Lincoln, and now he's pushing us to double output. This is how people get caught. It's also how people get hurt—namely me—when I have to rush to meet the new quota. This stuff is half a step away from blowing up through most of every batch. If I screw up ever so slightly, the barge and I will go *boom*."

Now Ben looked concerned. "You been lookin' more an' more tired, Greg. Ya know, ain't nothin' worth bein' kilt over."

"Thanks, little brother."

"No, I mean it! We kin do other stuff. I mean, yeah, this money's nice, but we cain't spend it nowhere 'thout worryin' 'bout gettin' caught, so, what good is it?"

Greg smiled. He had worried about having this same conversation with Ben, but now his brother had brought it up first. "I'm glad we both agree on this. How would you feel about getting a bigger barge, bigger tug, and a bigger crane, plus the rest of the equipment that we'll need to compete with the other marine contractors around the Chesapeake for the bigger, more profitable jobs? We're only a little bit shy on the amount of cash we'll need, and I figure another month of cooking this stuff, and that'll give us a good safety margin. Plus, I've got a plan for disguising where the money came from, so we'll be good on that aspect."

"Whatever you say, Greg." Then Ben grinned.

"What's that look for?"

"It'll be nice not ta have ta wake up an' worry every day, like ah do now."

This statement surprised Greg, who thought that he was the only one who felt this way. He smiled at his brother. "Yeah, it will. Plus, it'll be nice to get back to having good, clean money to spend and save. So, one more month and we call it quits?" He held up a fist and leaned over toward where Ben was sitting.

"Hell, yeah!" He bumped his fist with his brother's.

Friday, before dawn, at the rendezvous point...

The Captain pulled up and tied the skiff alongside the tug as the brothers came out of the wheelhouse to help. Then, the three went back inside to make the exchange, away from any possibility of prying eyes.

As they swapped the bags of cash and drugs, Greg said, "Captain, you know I was only going to stand in for Jeff for a couple of weeks before he got killed. I only kept going because it was easy money, and I still had a life. But now, that's come to an end since this guy Lincoln has come into the picture. With him wanting more and more territory, how long do you think it's going to take before he comes back at you wanting even more product?"

"Well, Greg, ya said it yourself, ya still got a life. An' I got one, too. But I dunno fer how long if we start tellin' Big Lincoln 'no.' He ain't one that takes kindly ta that, an' you know what? I ain't either. So, you jus' relax, an' keep doin' what yer doin' an' it'll all be good."

"That's just the thing, Captain, I can't relax anymore. I'll tell you what I'll do. I'll keep producing for four more weeks, and then that's it; I'm done."

The Captain's eyes bored into Greg's. He took his index finger and poked it into Greg's chest. "You'll be through when I tell ya you are, an' not afore. You got me?"

"Are you threatening me?"

"You catch on quick."

"I could just as easily make a batch that'll make your customers sick, you know."

"An' I could hurt you jus' as bad. So, why don' we jes' stop alla this talk 'bout quittin' an' let's keep makin' money."

"Four weeks, Captain. Then I'm out."

"We'll see 'bout that. Jus' get back ta cookin'. I gotta get goin' an' meet up wit' Big Lincoln. Ah'll see ya here on Tuesday."

The brothers watched the Captain leave, and they got underway after his boat went out of sight.

"Whatta ya think, Greg?"

"I think I'm glad he doesn't know where we live. And I also think we're going to bring guns with us on Tuesday. It doesn't appear that he's going to take our four weeks' notice seriously, and we might have to convince him about how real that deadline is."

THE CAPTAIN WAS deep in thought as he made his way down the Inside Passage in the skiff. Greg seriously wanting out wasn't something that the Captain had figured on before today. If he knew where they lived, he could sneak up on them and probably force Greg to keep producing. The same way he'd forced that site foreman to give up the location of that backpack of cash after he'd followed him home.

Cutting off fingers and making small cuts in tender places was an effective, though distasteful, way to get people to do things they wouldn't ordinarily want to do. But since he had to keep meeting both of those brothers together out on the water, that made things more difficult. There was no way to split them up, especially since now that they'd had this disagreement, he knew they would be more cautious.

While he didn't fully trust Big Lincoln, they both had a common interest in keeping Greg producing. He made up his mind to talk to Lincoln about it when he made the drop at the dock. Since the product was all going to one place, Lincoln had decided he didn't need to have the refrigerated trucks bring it to him in Richmond. Instead, he and his driver had started making the pickups at the Captain's dock on the west side of the bay. He could talk to him there.

As he approached the turn that would take him past *Mallard Cove*, he saw some guy on the flybridge of a sportfish inside a small cove getting all worked up and flipping him off. He couldn't hear over his old motor what the guy was apparently shouting at him. He started to slow down to confront the guy, but then he remembered the product he was carrying and went back to cruising speed. He didn't understand the guy's problem since he was on the other side of a rock jetty that protected a narrow inlet, and any wake he was making couldn't reach him. Besides, his small wake wouldn't have budged the big boat the guy was on.

He resisted the urge to flip him off in return, so instead, he ignored him. That's when it hit him that it was the guy who had free spooled all that line on his prop yesterday. The fact that the guy's other boat was right there on the shore of the route he had to use to pick up twice a week bothered him. He used the deadrise to try and blend in, not to draw attention to himself. It was identical to dozens of other deadrise outboard center consoles on the Chesapeake, yet this guy had recognized him. That wasn't good.

As he left the guy in his wake, he made the curve and headed for Fisherman Inlet Bridge. The Captain thought about how fast today had gone downhill. He hoped it wouldn't get any worse.

THE CAPTAIN WAS SITTING in Big Lincoln's car, swapping parcels, the drugs for cash. Big Lincoln scrunched up his nose. "Man, you smell like fish! Get th' hell outta mah car!"

"I was onna workboat, what'd ya expect?"

"Well, wash th' sumbitch next time! Don't be gettin' back in mah car smellin' like that again."

"Never mind that, we got a problem."

"Whatcha mean we?"

"As in you an' me. Us. Greg an' his brother wan' out, in four weeks."

"So, handle it."

"He won' lissen ta me. Got his mind set on it."

Big Lincoln leaned in closer to the Captain, and with a very menacing look, he repeated, with much emphasis, "So. Handle. It. You th' damn middleman; you suppose ta keep yo' boys in check. Why you think you gettin' a cut? Ta be ah damn water taxi?"

"Ahm gonna need your help. Ride wit' me next run. Ah cain't keep eyes on botha them at th' same time."

Instantly, Lincoln knew what had to be done. He sighed a theatrical sigh, then said, "Okay. I'll go on Tuesday. But jus' ta show ya how it's done. Now, get outta mah car afore I gotta get the interior detailed."

As the big black SUV pulled away from the fish house, Big Lincoln told his driver, "We got a trip ta make to th' Eastern Shore tonight. Get us some wheels won't nobody recognize. A van, an' put somethin' ta wrap his ass up in it. Ahm gonna teach that boy a lesson. If ya work fo' me, ya take care ah bidness on ya own. I ain't nobody's daddy what gonna hold they damn hand."

"Right, boss. I'll take care of it."

BALONEY WAS SURPRISED to see his "buddy" in the deadrise skiff going past *Casey's Cove* again this early. He jumped up from his captain's chair, spilling his hot coffee on his lap while emphatically flipping the guy off and making verbal comments about his obvious canine heritage. Never mind the fact that the motor was so loud and the distance far enough that there was no way the man could hear him.

For a second, it looked like the guy was going to stop, but then he kept on going. The man had definitely seen him, though, so he'd gotten his point across. Now Baloney climbed down the bridge ladder and went into the cabin for a fresh pair of pants and another coffee, all the while cursing the man under his breath.

14

KC'S PALS

F riday night at the Captain's home.

"AH KNEW you'd tell me what I wanna know—that you'd be reasonable, Captain," Big Lincoln said as he stood over the man. The Captain had been duct-taped into a chair and then beaten; Lincoln and his driver had each taken turns until they had gotten the information out of him. It hadn't taken long. While he put up a good tough-guy front at first, like so many guys who act tough, the Captain was more of a pushover when faced with violence.

"I bet them boys'd be upset knowin' how much you been markin' up they product. Ah know I am. Fifty damn percent, jes' fo' bringin' it 'cross th' bay, an' droppin' it off. Damn, boy!" He turned toward a closet where his driver was busy removing a bunch of junk that was blocking a small hidden door on the back wall. He finally got it open, revealing piles of cash rolls.

"Boss, you gonna wanna see this."

Lincoln switched places with him, whistling when he saw how many rolls were inside. He said to the Captain, "Damn, boy, you been at it fo' a while, ain'tcha?" He wasn't expecting so much cash to be here. "Wit' alla this, I'da figured ya woulda least bought ah new engine fo' that scow ya got. Damn!"

The Captain wasn't up for answering since they had duct-taped his mouth now, too. He knew that since they had figured out where he lived, they probably knew where Greg and Ben lived as well. Lincoln was here because he no longer needed the Captain. Once he'd given them the location of the cash, he knew what was coming.

Lincoln stuffed much of the cash into a black backpack, and the rest went into two large cardboard boxes from the closet. They had held mostly junk, stuff with no value other than camouflaging the hidden door. It was all dumped out on the floor in front of the closet. Now, Lincoln had his driver carry the boxes and the bag out to the van. While his driver was outside, Lincoln took his silenced .22 caliber pistol and shot the Captain in both the forehead and the heart. When the driver came back in, the two men cut the body loose and rolled it up in black plastic before taking it out to the van.

On the way back to the CBBT, they took an overgrown side road that led far back into the woods. Using the pair of shovels they'd brought with them, they dug a shallow grave in the soft earth, dumping the body in and covering it over. At some point, it might be dug up by animals, but it would be long after the Captain had been all but forgotten about.

SITTING in the dark in the open cockpit of her sailboat, Sally sipped her wine, thinking and planning through a fog of alcohol. Surprisingly, she had come to some logical conclusions. She knew now that the weather was getting warmer, the weekend business at *Mallard Cove* was picking up. The restaurants and bars there would be busy now through Monday morning, with many people anxious to get out of the cities and onto their boats for the weekend, some staying over Sunday night and leaving early on Monday. Not good timing for what she had in mind.

There was no way of getting into the little cove without being seen, so that was out. She also knew that Casey had liked taking early morning walks around *Bayside* on Tuesdays in the cooler weather of spring and fall. He liked checking on things before everything opened for the day. He was obsessive about all the details; at least, he had been back then. She was willing to bet he still was. She was also willing to bet that he would recognize her sailboat and want to see why it would be there and who was aboard.

The two of them had spent so much time together on it and made so many memories together. Then that damn redhead had wrecked everything, taking everything away from her. And now she had a kid, ensuring her claim to his money, no matter what. But paybacks are hell, bitch, and Sally had waited for far too long for Casey to wake up and come back. So long that she didn't want him back now. What she did want was revenge. To cause Dawn as much pain as she'd caused Sally. And there was that damned Murphy. He'd have nothing today without Casey having led him around by the hand.

No, everything revolved around Casey. If he was taken out of the picture, that whole group would fall apart. And that was exactly what Sally had in mind. But the timing would be crucial, and she had a plan. Now, she just needed a little luck.

CASEY WAS RESTLESS. Dawn had already fed Summer; then, at nine o'clock, after having a glass of wine, she'd gone to bed, knowing she would need to get up and feed her again in a few hours. Sitting in the salon, the boat was deathly quiet. Andrea was the crewmember on duty, but her main responsibility after dinner was to be on hand to call for help in case of water intrusion or fire. She was around but steered clear, giving the Shaws their privacy.

This was the time of year when the hours after twilight became chilly, perfect for a fire in the stone fire pit at *C2*. Casey put on a light jacket and headed down the dock.

As he passed the boats of his friends, he was pleased with how

Casey's Cove had evolved. Not just the structures but the friends it had attracted. Actually, that wasn't right, he thought. This group of people was a large part of the attraction; otherwise, it would be a very lonely marina ghost town. It was kind of like the *Lady Dawn* right now. It was still an elegant yacht, but with Dawn and Summer asleep and none of their friends on board, it was a very lonely place.

That was the thing about a fire pit: you might be the only one around it, but it never felt lonely, at least until that last piece burned down to ash and coals. Casey took his time, shaping the perfect pyre with split hardwood. After seeing it start, he grabbed a beer from the mini fridge and kicked back in a lounge chair.

He'd no sooner settled in than he heard Baloney ask, "Mind some company, Case?"

"Company would be good, Bill. Grab a beer and a chair." He said this despite knowing that Baloney was going to do it anyway.

As he sat down, Baloney said, "You're in ah funny mood there, Case. Callin' me Bill, ah mean."

"Oh, I didn't even realize that I had. Sorry, Baloney."

"Nah, it's good. Ya know, that's all Betty ever called me, an' I kinda miss it sometimes. 'Course I miss her alla time."

His wife of more than three decades, Betty, had been murdered last summer, and Baloney had been critically injured by the attacker. Everyone here in the *Cove* had done their best to keep him occupied once he had gotten out of the hospital. The couple had been living aboard *My Mahi* on *Mallard Cove*'s charter boat row when the attack occurred, waiting for *Dorado*'s renovations to be completed. Casey had rushed to get the new slip built in time for it to arrive a few days before Baloney's release.

"We all do, though you miss her more, obviously. She was such a sweet woman."

"Yeah." He took a sip of beer and then concentrated on the flames that were steadily building. "You're ah good friend, Casey. I never did thank ya for buildin' that slip for me an' gettin' *Dorado* all ready for me ta move in, but I appreciate it. I'd ah hated ta have ta go back ta *Mahi* or back over by th' charter boats. So many memories, ya know?"

"Yeah, Bill, I do. No thanks needed, I'm glad we could get everything ready for you in time to come home. Nice to see you out fishing again now, too."

"Yeah, that was fun. An' speakin' ah that, the sumbitch that cost me th' biggest blue an' ah spool ah line? That guy inna deadrise wit' th' old engine? He's come by here ah few times, inna ditch. I let 'im know what I thought 'bout it this mornin' in sign language."

"You waved at him?"

"Yeah, I waved. I jus' didn't use alla my fingers." Baloney laughed, recalling the event. "But I wonder what he's doin' aroun' here? Maybe he docks up the way? I seen him right at daylight."

"No clue, Bill. But I doubt he'll come around here now that he knows he's not welcome."

"Yeah. I sure told 'im."

"What are you guys cooking?" Sandy and KC, the cat, rounded the corner of the boathouse.

"We're not cookin', we're drinkin'. Grab a brew an' cop ah squat."

"Gilligan, the damage you do to the English language would send my proofreader into therapy."

Baloney snorted. "Ah jus' talk like people talk, not like that stuff in yer books. All 'hoidy toidy.' Real people don' talk like that, ya hack."

"Whatever. It sells, which is why I could repay some of Casey's beer the other day. What's your excuse?"

"I do my share."

"Hah! Since when?"

"Whenever anybody brings beer ta th' boat, an' I got a full fridge, I put it in here!"

"In other words, never."

"It happens!"

"You forgot a couple of consonants on that first word."

"Huh?"

"That's not them."

Casey realized he needed to head off this confrontation before it got more intense. "Hey, KC, where have you been?"

The cat came over and jumped up beside Casey, wanting to get petted. Casey was what the cat deemed a "fish provider," which put him high on his list of good humans. Casey always set aside a generous quantity of "cat tax" when he cleaned fish. Though Casey was more of a dog person, KC was his main feline exception. The cat settled in on his lap.

"Don't go stealing my cat, Casey."

"No chance of that, Sandy. He's just repaying all that mackerel I gave him."

"Hey! Youse give that cat whatever he wants. Ah owe him mah life. An' if ya run outta fish ta give him, ah'll run ta th' market an' get some. That cat is aces."

KC looked over at Baloney, his coat glistening and eyes glowing in the firelight. There was clearly a bond between the two, not unlike the one he shared with Casey. KC had been out on a nightly prowl in the predawn hours when he had seen Baloney sprawled on his deck in a pool of blood with a knife sticking out of his chest. The cat had run back to Sandy's boat, waking him up and using his claws to get Sandy's attention, then led him to Baloney like a feline Lassie.

So, Baloney wasn't kidding; the cat had saved his life. Of course, convincing law enforcement that this is what happened took a lot of work, along with a review of *Casey's Cove*'s security camera recordings. With Sandy and Baloney's long, and sometimes almost heated, history of bickering over bar tabs, the cops had "liked" Sandy for the crime at first.

Eventually, the killer was brought to justice (as in, no longer breathing), and things around *Mallard Cove* settled back to normal. At least, as normal as it got around there.

The conversation died down as they all became somewhat mesmerized by the flames. There was something about having a beer with friends around a fire on a chilly, early spring night that was very comforting. No matter if you were by the ocean or in the woods; it created a deeper, silent bond between friends, either new or old.

Finally, Casey became the first to leave, feeling slightly guilty for being there without Dawn. KC then switched over to Baloney's lap, something he'd have never done before the attack. Fifteen minutes later, when Sandy stood up to go, KC looked at Baloney, who said, "Yeah, go on, pal. Somebody's gotta make sure that th' old hack gets home okay. Ahm jus' gonna finish this beer."

As if understanding what his friend said, KC jumped down and passed Sandy on the way back to the boat, looking back a couple of times to make sure his human roommate was still in tow.

Baloney watched the fire until there were no more flames nor beer, just coals and an empty bottle. He thought about how all his friends had stuck around him as he recuperated and how lucky he was to have them so close by. Without them here, he wondered how he would've been able to get his head mostly back on straight. Even now, going back to an empty boat was tough.

At least it was a different boat, without anything to remind him of Betty other than a few pictures and knickknacks, plus his own memories of a life so well spent together. Now in his early fifties, he wondered how many more springs he would have to endure alone before it was his turn to join her. While everyone thought he was healed, it was those wounds you can't see that were the worst. He stood up and trudged back to his boat.

THE NEXT MORNING, Baloney started the day with his now usual routine of a cup of coffee on the flying bridge. Only today, there was no sign of the loud wooden skiff by the time he'd reached the bottom of his mug. Normally, he would go back down to the galley and cook his breakfast, but today, he didn't feel like eating alone. He rinsed his mug, then started walking over to the *Cove* restaurant. Even though he'd still be eating alone there, at least he'd have people around him. He'd still have to pass *My Mahi*, where the attack happened, but it was becoming less and less difficult.

A few months ago, he had considered selling it, but then he couldn't bear to sign the brokerage's listing contract. It was another boat that he and Betty had fixed up together and then lived aboard for a couple of seasons. Plus, he'd made it famous on *Tuna Hunters*.

But due to his injuries, he'd missed last year. He was planning on being in it and fishing this year, though.

His thoughts were interrupted when he spotted Murph and Lindsay stepping ashore from their house barge, apparently having the same plan for breakfast.

"Hey Baloney! Going over for breakfast?" Lindsay asked.

"Yeah. Youse guys?"

"Uh-huh. Join us?"

He smiled. "Yeah, sure." He loved calling them "the kids," even though they weren't all that young. It was one of what had come to be referred to as a "Baloneyism." He had been the first to sign a contract for a slip when they bought the marina. Back then, the docks had been falling in at some spots, and several slips were vacant because they were missing pilings. The only restaurant on-site was closed, and the building was dilapidated.

The pair had used up all of their savings to buy the place, and Cetta used some underhanded tactics to try to get the seller to break his contract with them, and instead sell to him. It had ended up with Cetta getting a butt full of lead, not from a firearm, but from a pitching arm. After he refused to leave their property, Lindsay had tossed a few large egg-shaped lead fishing weights at Cetta's backside and Range Rover's roof. There'd been no love lost between the pair and him since then.

After closing on the property deal, they intended to invest their meager future profits in repairs and improvements over the next several years. But Casey approached them about him and Dawn becoming partners and making the needed repairs immediately. Murph was reluctant, but Lindsay talked him into it, and it turned out to be the best move.

Baloney had been apprehensive about the changes, though he didn't mind not having to step over the holes in the docks any longer. Then he became a big fan when his charter bookings picked up dramatically when more and more people discovered *Mallard Cove*.

Within a few months, the newly renovated restaurant was being expanded, then the back deck was added, and a hotel and the first beach bar were under construction. The place became a gold mine for the partners, and they soon began adding additional properties around the Chesapeake.

As they walked across the marina, Baloney smiled and chuckled softly.

Lindsay asked, "What's funny?"

"Jes' thinkin' back on youse two when ya bought this place. Whatta dump! But ya knew what it could be, an' I'm glad ya did. If Cetta had got ahold ah it, it'd still be ah dump."

Murph said, "Which is why I'm so glad he's not going to be across the road. So far, we've been able to get the better of him every time. I hope it stays that way."

"I hope we never cross paths again," Lindsay said.

"Yeah, so does he, ah bet!" Baloney laughed, as the others joined in. He was glad he'd decided not to cook; he loved their company, and the feeling was mutual.

15

CITATION TIME

When the trio got to the charter dock, both of Baloney's boats were still in their slips, idling and warming up their engines. Baloney spotted Bobby, who used to be his mate on the *Golden Dolphin*, but now ran *My Mahi* for him. He was also his first mate during the filming of *Tuna Hunters*.

"Whatcha got goin' today, Bobby?"

"Two full-day charters. Macks and blues are at the mouth of the bay, so I figure we'll start there, and then run offshore a ways and see if we can't luck into some tuna."

"How's th' rest ah th' week lookin'?"

"One boat tomorrow, and two on Friday. You know how it is preseason. But future bookings are looking up starting in two weeks.

"Good deal. Well, good luck, an' catch 'em up! An' if ya run inta tuna, gimme a call."

"Roger that, Cap. We'll do our best."

ONCE INSIDE, the trio picked a table by the windows overlooking the deck and the charter boats. They were still studying the menus when Sandy walked up.

"You guys didn't feel like cooking either?"

"Grab a chair, Hack! An' nah, it's not worth messin' up th' galley every day for one person. Kinda nice ta have company, too."

"Not to mention, then you have more people you can stick the tab with, too, Gilligan!"

At the mention of his dreaded nickname, Baloney frowned and looked around at the other occupied tables. "Not in mixed company, ya hack! An' I ain't stickin' none of youse wit' th' tab. In fact, ahm buyin' breakfast fer alla yas."

His three companions all looked at each other in shock. Sandy said, "You aren't sick, are you?"

"What! Can't ah guy buy his friends ah bite ta eat?"

"Of course, you can, but it usually comes with a catch. You don't need a ride to Delaware or something heavy moved, right?" Sandy was only half kidding.

"Sheesh! You've been writin' too many crime books; yer suspicious ah everybody. An' no, ah don't. I just been thinkin' 'bout how much I appreciate youse three. It's nice ta have friends, ya know?"

Lindsay reached over and put her hand on his arm as she smiled, touched by the sentiment. "Yes, we do know."

Baloney subconsciously looked out the window at the *Mahi*, as she was pulling out of the slip, and into the cockpit where he came so close to dying last year. Then he looked back at his friends and nodded and smiled.

THE RESTAURANT HAD a ten-minute wait for tables by the time they all left. It was early in the season for that—hopefully a good sign for a strong upcoming summer.

Sandy said he was going to go write on his back deck, and the Murphys said they were going to do some cleaning on *LNZ II*. Baloney went back to *Dorado*, and got busy checking his tackle, just in case Bobby called. He hadn't pulled on any tuna since the attack. It had taken quite a while for some of the injured muscles to heal enough that he could be up to the task. Tuna pulled like small locomotive engines, and they could wear out even the most fit angler.

A little before eleven, Bobby called and said they were on some yellowfin in close, feeding on schools of small herring. He figured it would take Bill half an hour to reach him.

Baloney cranked his engines then leaned out over the gunwale and shouted to Sandy, "Yellowfin! Ya in, Hack?"

"On my way, Gilligan!"

Murph and Lindsay were both looking at Baloney from *LNZ II*. Baloney yelled, "What? Youse two need ah engraved invitation? Let's go!"

Murph and Lindsay hurried around to the big Merritt boat that they had once owned before Baloney bought it at a fire sale. A *literal* fire sale, after the wheelhouse had been burned, which was a story for another day. He had it rebuilt at a friend's boatyard just a couple of miles away, the same boatyard where he had rebuilt *My Mahi*, which he had bought when it was underwater. Literally, as in sunk. The 'yard had done such a good job on *Dorado* that she looked like the day she was launched down in Florida.

One of the advantages of the four of them fishing together was that they had all fished professionally at one time or another. Sandy had been a backcountry guide down in Islamorada in the Florida Keys. Murph and Lindsay had been one of the hottest tournament charter crews on the East Coast and had fished *Dorado* when she'd belonged to them and was called *Irish Luck*. Baloney, of course, had been a charter boat captain at *Mallard Cove*.

This meant that as a crew, they required little to no direction; they all knew their jobs. Not that this meant Baloney wouldn't still yell orders, which went largely ignored. Lindsay started the generator and unhooked the shore power cord then untied the spring line as Sandy cast off the stern line. Murph got the bow line, dropping it onto the floating dock as they pulled out of the slip.

As Baloney eased out into "the ditch," Baloney half expected to see that old deadrise skiff coming around the bend, but it didn't happen. He was soon joined on the flybridge by the three others. He had a huge grin on his face as he lit his cigar.

"Ya know this's th' first time I've had *Dorado* out. Glad youse guys'r wit' me."

This made quite an impact on his friends. None of them had realized this before Baloney pointed it out, but it was true. He was still in the hospital when a group of them had ferried the boat from the boatyard to her new slip. Then they'd stocked her and made her ready for Baloney's arrival. They'd taken turns helping him with things like grocery shopping and other errands until he could go solo. He hadn't recovered enough yet to fish before winter set in, so *Dorado* had stayed in the slip until today.

The enormity of this event had slipped their minds until now, and it wasn't the only milestone they'd missed. They suddenly realized that their run down the coast the other day had been Baloney's first boat ride since that fateful day. Ordinarily, they would have expected him to make a big deal over it, but he hadn't. Now they understood how emotional it must've been for him, and keeping that to himself was not what they'd have expected. He hadn't wanted it to be obvious.

Lindsay asked, "Is that the first time you've lit a cigar since..."

Baloney nodded and gave her a sad smile, then softly said, "Yeah, since I lost Betty. Ya know, that was ah strict rule wit' her; ah can't light up 'till ah clear th' jetties when ahm out fishin'. Not changin' that feels kinda like it keeps ah part ah her still alive, ya know?"

Lindsay fought almost successfully to keep her voice from cracking. "Then, don't you dare change that, Bill."

At a very rare loss for words, Bill simply nodded. Then he pushed the throttles forward, bringing the Merritt up to a fast cruising speed as Murph lowered the aluminum outriggers into their trolling positions. They all rode in silence for another ten minutes.

Baloney checked the radar, seeing a small group of strong returns about twelve miles ahead. Apparently, some other boats had joined Bobby on his tuna school. He then dropped the radar's range down a bit to make it more powerful closer to their boat. It was one thing to join "the fleet" on a school of tuna, but it was even better to find your own school, one that might've been overlooked. If you had it all to yourself, you didn't need to be concerned with running over someone else's lines or having them get in your way when you were fighting a fish, like had happened with his bluefish.

A few minutes later, he spotted some faint returns on the screen, which was exactly what he'd hoped for. The radar had picked up a scattered group of birds working a bait school a few miles away from Bobby.

Murph was looking over his shoulder and saw the same thing. Baloney said, "Bobby said he's on ah school ah herring."

Murph replied, "Got it." This helped Murph decide what bait selection he would use. Then, he hurried down the ladder to begin readying the rods and baits.

Baloney smiled widely as he told the others, "Birds. An' we got 'em all ta ourself." Without a word, Lindsay and Sandy also climbed down to help Murph, leaving Baloney puffing away on that first cigar.

Normally, tuna were found about sixty miles or so offshore in the canyons. This was the area where the continental shelf dropped off steeply, but instead of having a straight edge, there were almost fingers of shallower ridges with deep crevices in between. After the bait "runs" inshore petered out, these canyons held smaller groups of bait, attracting tuna, billfish, and other gamefish. But right now, the huge bait schools were closer to shore, attracted by specific temperatures as the seasonal change took place. These tuna preferred a certain temperature, too, which often coincided with what the bait schools followed. Until the warmer water moved in for the summer in a few weeks, it wouldn't be that uncommon to find these schools closer to shore.

Baloney squinted at the horizon, hoping to see the birds. A couple of minutes later, he did. A large group of storm petrels, otherwise known as tuna birds. He began throttling back as he neared the area where they were diving. A group of feeding porpoises rolled around them, and there was a small oil slick on the surface. Herring were very oily fish, and as they were injured by predators, they would lose enough oil to create a slick. Porpoises were also great for finding bait schools. With their highly attuned sonar, they could locate schools up to two miles away.

Suddenly, the tuna's feeding frenzy ignited, and several broke the surface while chasing the herring. Others literally launched themselves out of the water in a display of pelagic aerobatics as they focused on the much smaller herring, about six inches long.

Murph and Lindsay each picked up a rod and dropped their baits back past the white water boiling up behind the stern. Sandy stood ready with his rod, waiting to drop his bait in until both of those lines were run through the outrigger clips and then hoisted up and away from the boat. As Murph went to place his line in the clip, it was torn from his fingers, and suddenly, the reel started screaming.

"Fish on, Baloney!" Murph picked up the rod from its holder in the gunwale's teak covering board and placed the butt in the gimbal of his fighting belt. The line continued to stream out as he began applying pressure with the rod.

Lindsay was running her line up the outrigger when its clip made a resounding snapping sound. She called out, "Doubled up," and also used her fishing belt to start fighting the tuna while standing up.

Baloney had put both transmissions in neutral until he could see which direction each fish would take. Both had sounded, but neither fish had yet picked a direction other than down to get away from the boat. The danger here was they were so close together that the lines could touch and chafe, risking breaking both lines. Baloney now bumped both transmissions into forward, trying to get more of an angle on the lines. Hopefully, this would encourage the fish to swim away from each other. The line loss began to slow as the reels' drags began taking more effect. Lindsay had been on the port corner of the cockpit, but now her fish began crossing over toward Murph's.

Baloney bellowed, "They're gonna cross! Switch sides. Lindsay, go under Murph's line."

She ducked down under Murph's rod, swapping corners with her husband. Now Baloney began paying attention to who was more able to begin retrieving their line. Sandy would man the gaff whenever the time came, and that large Merritt cockpit would soon look a lot smaller as fish came over the side.

The ballet was on as the anglers fought for footing and balance in the three-foot rollers. Not enough wave action to be uncomfortable, but just enough to take away some of your balance at the wrong time.

Twenty minutes later, with Sandy on the gaff, Lindsay landed a forty-pounder. Five minutes later, Murph boated a thirty-pounder.

Sandy beamed. "KC is going to eat well tonight!"

Murph went over to Lindsay and whispered in her ear. She got a big, lopsided grin and nodded. Then Murph climbed the bridge ladder and went over to Baloney.

"Get your butt down to where the action is, Cap. Time for you to get on some fish."

Baloney was taken aback for a second, then said, "Ya know, I wouldn' let jus' anybody take th' wheel, ya know. But seein' as you used ta own her, I guess I kin trust ya!" He winked and was down the ladder in a shot to take the place of an angler.

At Murph's suggestion, Lindsay had broken out a couple of the smaller mackerel they had saved from last week's fishing. She put one on each rod.

Baloney was surprised. "Ain't those kinda big?"

"Want to catch big fish? Use big bait!" Lindsay laughed at her own saying.

Murph scanned the surface with binoculars, looking for signs of the now-disappeared bait school. Then, a quarter-mile away, he spotted a disturbance on the water's surface. He increased speed slightly and called down to the cockpit, "Six hundred yards; get ready!"

The timing, once again, couldn't have been better. The surface exploded just as their lines reached the froth. The left rigger clicked a second or two before the right one. Judging from the bend on the starboard rod, that fish was a horse. Lindsay directed Bill, "Get in the fighting chair!"

"Ah was gonna stand-up fight."

"Not with this fish, you weren't!" She waited until he was in the chair before she passed him the rod loaded with fifty-pound test line.

Once he felt the pulling strength of the fish, he said, "Ah think you're right. This one's a hoss!"

"Sandy, are you set?" Lindsay asked.

"All good! This one doesn't feel nearly as big as the one Bill's got."

The grin on Baloney's face couldn't get much larger. Cigar smoke was coming out of his mouth in puffs, reminding Sandy of a steam engine. He was using the footrest for leverage on what was obviously a very good fish.

Lindsay backed away from each angler and began texting on her phone. After several exchanges, she smiled broadly, then looked up at Murph. He was turned around backward, facing the cockpit in the typical captain's fish-fighting position. Ignoring the wheel, he was using both throttle/gear levers from behind his back to be able to point the stern at the fish. He glanced at Lindsay, who held up her phone and a thumbs up. He grinned back at her, then went back to concentrating on the fight, one deck below him.

Sandy's fish came in twenty minutes later, weighing fifty-two pounds. "Well, that was fun. Think yours will top mine, Gilligan?"

Baloney was sweating and grunting; the cigar stub, having been allowed to burn out, was perched in the corner of his mouth. "Th' tail ah mine'll outweigh yer whole fish!"

It would take another twenty-five minutes before they would know for certain. But then it took Lindsay and Sandy both pulling together to be able to haul the fish through the transom door; they saw it was an obvious citation fish. The lower limit for a citation yellowfin was seventy pounds.

Murph leaned over the back flybridge rail. "Y'all had enough, or do you want to catch some more?"

Baloney was still in the chair, catching his breath. He put one arm up in the air. "Ahm good."

They all laughed. Sandy said, "I'm with Gilligan on this. If y'all want a few more, we can go for it."

"I think we have enough, babe. We have a lot of boat to wash, and fish to clean. Not to mention a citation to weigh," Lindsay said.

"Murph, ya wanna run yer ol' boat in? I kinda like th' view from down here right now."

Baloney wasn't fooling anyone; he was setting up a grand entrance back at *Mallard Cove*, sitting in the fighting chair when they backed into the scale's slip to weigh the tuna. There was going to be no doubt about who the angler actually was.

"I'll be happy to...Captain Gilligan!"

16

SURPRISE

Murph had radioed ahead to *Mallard Cove*, and Barry Rolle, the dockmaster, was standing by at the scale when Murph brought *Dorado* in and spun her around, backing into the slip at the base of the center dock. A small crowd had gathered, many of them tourists, curious about what was going on. A murmur started when they opened the huge chill box under the cockpit deck, and they saw the size of the largest fish.

Barry, who was originally from The Bahamas, said loudly with his Bahamian accent, "Mon, dat t'ing ah citation fo' shore!" He was enhancing his accent for the benefit of the tourists.

Barry swung the boom from the steel pipe gantry out over the boat's cockpit. He lowered the block and tackle's electronic scale with its hook and tail rope, already zeroed out and ready to weigh the fish. He hoisted the tuna and swung it over in front of the gantry with all its *Mallard Cove* signage. A sandwich board was all filled out with *Dorado*'s name, Baloney as the angler, Murph as the captain, and Lindsay and Sandy as the mates. It had a space left open for the weight.

Barry studied the readout. "One hundred forty-seven pounds, even!"

Baloney's "crew" all high-fived their angler, and all four got out to pose for the obligatory publicity photos. This early in the season, these shots would go a long way to building traffic on the charter dock.

Since he was a cable TV celebrity, Baloney posed for photos with numerous tourists next to his fish. He might have missed the last filming season but was still as popular as ever.

Half an hour later, they loaded the tuna back into the cockpit for the short ride to *Casey's Cove* and a date with the *C2* cleaning table. Though no one had told him, KC was waiting at Baloney's slip. It was funny how some cats knew things.

"KC, mah little pal, ah gotcha plenny ah tuna!" Baloney smiled at his furry savior.

KC leaped up onto the covering board, apparently to supervise the unloading. No human had ever looked at a Kobe beef steak with as much anticipation as that cat did when he eyed those fish. They loaded the tuna onto a dock cart, and Murph wheeled them to the cleaning table with KC hot on his heels. Sandy, Lindsay, and Murph hoisted the big fish onto the table first while Baloney supervised, beer already in hand. KC was now perched on a shelf at the end of the table, waiting on the feline version of tuna poké.

Lindsay and Sandy had used the boat's freshwater system to wash the rods, tackle, flybridge, and most of the cockpit on the way back into the dock, leaving only the foredeck, wheelhouse, and hull all that remained to be washed. Lindsay and Sandy were done well before Murph was halfway through cleaning the tuna and paying the "cat tax." Baloney stayed busy supervising, of course.

As Murph got close to the end of cleaning the last tuna, Lindsay sent another text. Five minutes later, she distracted Baloney until he heard "Surprise!" from a group of people behind him who had all gathered to celebrate his return to fishing. They brought side dishes to go with the tuna that would be grilled. There was even a cake with an icing rendition of him pulling on his tuna from *Dorado*, which had been quickly decorated at the *Mallard Cove's* restaurant after Dawn had received Lindsay's first text.

In addition to Casey, Dawn, and Summer, Kari and Marlin Denton were there. The last pair were partners in the property investment group; Kari also ran the property management and acquisitions. Marlin had a foundation dedicated to preserving mid-Atlantic fisheries and also owned the *Tuna Hunters* production company. They lived aboard their house barge, docked in the slip next to the Murphys. Standing behind them were "Rut" Rutledge and his girlfriend, Cammie Pinder. Rut owned *Mockhorn Boat Works* and managed a fund benefiting struggling watermen and their families, and Cammie was Kari's assistant.

Casey said, "Bill, I can't tell you how happy we all are to see you return to fishing again, and in typical form, you've done it with quite a splash!" He passed him a tablet that was opened to a local social media site that already had pictures of him with his fish.

While he loved seeing his picture online, seeing these friends all gathered to celebrate the last part of his recovery was almost too much for him. It became one of those rare occasions when Baloney was at a total loss for words. Almost. "Ah can't tell ya how much this means ta me..."

His words were interrupted by the sound of a helicopter, apparently inbound for landing on the pad beyond the pool. A large red and white Sikorsky executive helicopter settled on the concrete, and after the blades stopped turning, billionaire Eric Clarke and his mid-teen daughter, Missy, stepped out. Behind them was Eric's girlfriend, ex-Congresswoman Candi Ryan, plus Rikki Jenkens and her partner, Cindy Crenshaw. All but Missy and Candi were also investors in the property group.

The five had been at the group's *Bayside Resort* when Dawn called and told them about the party for Baloney and the tuna run. Eric and Casey owned *Sharke*, their seventy-foot Jarrett Bay sportfisherman. So Eric decided to kill two birds with one stone: attend the party today, stay overnight on the boat, and then take *Sharke* on a tuna hunt tomorrow.

As they joined the group gathered around Baloney, he glared at Eric and said, "Like ah was sayin' before 'Bucks' here interrupted me wit' that loud entrance, thank ya for this. All ah ya mean a lot ta me, an' I won't forget this an' alla th' visits when I was laid up, too. There's nobody I'd rather celebrate mah gettin' back onna water wit' than youse guys."

~

WHILE THE PARTY was going on at C2, a few miles away, Greg had finished up production for the day and was working on a different project. After having time to think it over, he figured that he wouldn't put it past the Captain and Big Lincoln not to take his four-week deadline seriously. He knew one thing that would: if all the components and equipment were destroyed.

He mixed up a powerful explosive compound that he placed next to the volatile chemicals he used to create the meth. He planned that after he made that last batch in four weeks, he would use the tug and push the barge over a deep section of the Inside Passage. Then, he would use a remote control to detonate the explosives. If he no longer had the setup, there was nothing the Captain could do to force them to continue. Big Lincoln would need to return to whoever made the crystal for him before Greg. Then, the brothers' lives would return to normal, and Greg was looking forward to it.

~

LATER THAT NIGHT, at Casey's Cove...

SANDY PUT one last piece of hardwood onto the fire before sitting down. Only he and Baloney were left; Murph and Lindsay had been the last ones of the others to turn in half an hour ago. The new piece caught fire, rekindling the dying fire.

"Ya know somethin', Sandy? I didn' realize how alone I'd been alla this winter, stayin' on board by myself. I miss Betty, an' ah guess ah tried ta wall myself off from th' rest ah th' world, 'cause there ain't nobody else like her. Never will be, neither.

"Seein' everybody together again tho', an realizin' how many friends ah got made me feel ah lot less alone, ya know? Boy, I never knew how much ah missed these cookouts an' everybody bein' aroun' here tugether. Even you, ya hack."

"Don't go getting all sentimental on me, Gilligan. Though you know, you're right. Everybody that was here would do anything for you. They're the true definition of 'friends.' You can count on all of us."

"Ah never did thank ya for savin' my life, did I?"

"Not necessary. I did what you would have done in a reverse situation."

"Okay, in that case, I won't thank ya." He grinned.

"I never thought you would," Sandy replied, laughing.

Baloney wanted to switch gears. "Gonna be different aroun' here, what wit' a couple ah kids growin' up."

"It is. But you know, I'm kind of looking forward to it. Yeah, it makes me feel a little older, but that's okay. Seeing a new generation coming along and them being able to grow up on the water, who wouldn't want that for their kids?

"I see it as an opportunity for us old farts to teach them respect for the dangers of the water and how to be good stewards of the bay and the ocean. That's the contribution I want to make. Plus, watching Casey and Murph teaching them how to fish and run boats will be fun."

"Yeah, I can't wait. That lil' Summer is already growin' like ah weed. Don' blink, or she'll be in college, an' we'll be ancient."

"True. But you know what? I think it will be worth that cost. Life is a ride, my friend. Jump in, sit down, and buckle up."

"Ya forgot th' 'an' shut up' part."

"Oh, like anything could shut you up? I wasn't going to waste my breath!"

"True, Hack, very true."

~

Murph again walked down the dock next to *Lady Dawn*. Casey saw him and motioned him aboard. As he got to the back deck, Casey motioned to a chair for him to sit.

"What, did you miss the boat?" *Sharke* had left half an hour earlier, right after sunrise.

"No, I had enough yesterday. Missy really wanted to fish with just the girls, and Eric was planning to work some in the salon while they were out, so I stayed on shore." *Sharke* had full satellite internet, giving him all the necessary connectivity to work until they got into the fish.

"Had breakfast yet?"

"Yeah, I made breakfast an hour and a half ago for me and Linds. But I could do with another cup of coffee."

Andrea had come out on deck after seeing Murph arrive. Casey had already had breakfast but liked coffee on the back deck on these cooler mornings. She nodded at Murph before disappearing inside. She reappeared a minute later with a cup for Murph and an insulated coffee carafe, filling Murph's cup and topping off Casey's before disappearing inside again.

Murph took a sip, then said, "I took a chance that you weren't on an inspection tour of the property."

"Season is starting, so there are already too many people around to do that on the weekends. Probably Tuesday if it's not raining."

"You are a creature of habit, Case."

"Oh, you weren't, back when you worked for me instead of with me like now?" He grinned, remembering their days in South Florida when Murph was his only employee and Casey had only a handful of properties. Murph had a set routine every week that he stuck to.

Murph grinned back. "True. But I've changed, and you haven't. Much. Speaking of change, where's your wife and daughter?"

"Sleeping in. The middle of the night feedings are brutal on Dawn, so I try to clear out early and quietly."

"Ah. I'm taking notes, so I know what to do in a few months."

"What to do is figure it out as you go along! Babies don't come with manuals; from what I hear, each one is different. I only know what works for us and Summer."

"Got it. I'm still getting used to this whole pregnancy thing."

"It doesn't get easier when they're born; there are just different types of challenges. You'll see."

"I'm good with challenges, but you know that about me. And now that I'm kind of over the shock of being pregnant, I'm looking forward to having a little one."

"Just remember, pal, if it's a boy, pack your bags!" Casey laughed at their new joke.

ABOARD SALLY'S SAILBOAT, she woke up with a piledriver inside her head. Her drinking had been increasing, though after today, she was going to have to slow way down. The plan was to leave the dock and motor down to *Mallard Cove* tomorrow night. She wanted to get in there late enough so the dockmaster would be gone. If everything went according to that plan, she'd be gone before he arrived for work, too. It all depended on whether Casey was still keeping the same schedule he used to back at *Bayside*. She was counting on that.

But for now, she wanted another drink, while she still could, to stop the pounding in her head.

THE TUNA HAD COOPERATED for *Sharke's* crew, and they had a fish box full, having reached their limit of three per person. Most were thirty to forty pounds, and only one approached the seventy-pound citation limit. No matter the size, they were all great fighters.

Eric wanted to take some home to Northern Virginia to give to friends and put several in his freezer. Rikki and Cindy also wanted to freeze some for themselves back at *Bayside*, where they lived aboard their Hatteras boat. One of the great things about yellowfin tuna, besides the great taste and texture, was that it was a sustainable resource with no sign of a dwindling population.

Midafternoon, Murph was waiting at the dock with the cart, though it would take two trips to the cleaning table to haul all the tuna. Missy and Lindsay helped with cleaning duty, which took much longer than the previous day but yielded many more pounds of tuna loins. Plus, they cut out many pounds of the lighter, more highly prized, fatty belly meat that was great for sushi and sashimi. KC, who was back on his shelf, wasn't that picky, taking whatever scraps were passed his way.

The helicopter returned to pick up its passengers after flying to the Accormack airport last night to be refueled and hangared. Once all five passengers had showered and changed, they loaded three big coolers filled with fish and climbed aboard after saying goodbye to their friends.

The Murphys and Shaws watched as the helicopter took off, banking over *Mallard Cove* before heading to the pad at *Bayside*. There, they would drop off one of the coolers and Rikki and Cindy before continuing to Eric's pad at his office/home. It sure beat fighting the Sunday auto exodus from the Eastern Shore since there were only two ways off and plenty of seasonal traffic.

Lindsay told Murph, "I'm tired. Mind if you cook tonight?"

"Even better, I'll pick up takeout from the *Cove*. You might not want to exert yourself so much in your condition." He looked worried.

"Oh, I'll keep fishing until I'm too big to go, which will be many months from now. Trust me, I'll know when to quit."

Dawn looked at her and silently nodded her support. She had done the same thing, fishing, until the last few months of her pregnancy. Both were tough women and good mothers.

17

NEW BOSS

M *onday, just before midnight at Mallard Cove...*

THE SAILBOAT *CREOLA* quietly motored into the *Mallard Cove Marina* basin. Sally picked out an open slip between two boats with brokerage signs since they wouldn't be occupied. She backed in and tied up to the floating finger pier next to a rear cabin powerboat with a raised rear deck with wraparound canvas and isinglass windows. This would give her a height advantage with cover and a good vantage point.

She had a short drink to steady her nerves, then climbed into her bunk on *Creola* and set her alarm for 5:00 a.m. Now, for some sleep before she had to get ready. Hopefully, Casey would keep to his old habits.

BIG LINCOLN'S driver had fortunately suggested that they leave early to go pick up the Captain's skiff since he'd seen there was a chance of fog this morning. The closer they got to the CBBT, the worse it was. On the bridge, as they crossed the water, in some places they couldn't see thirty feet.

"Boss, are you sure it's such a good idea for you to run that boat in this stuff? Maybe we should just go to they house an' do the pickup there. I mean, you don't have much boat experience…"

"Jus' shut up an' drive! I got all th' experience I need ta go meet up wit' them. An' they likely already out there. They expectin' that boat, an' if it don' show up, they might freak out or sompthin'. Ah caint take that chance. Ah'll go slow, an' stick to th' shoreline. Nothin' to it. Now, jus' keep yer eyes onna road."

CASEY WOKE up a few minutes before five, then quietly slipped out of bed and went down the hall to another stateroom where he'd temporarily put his clothes. He had been showering and dressing here since the baby had been born. He didn't want to risk waking either Summer or Dawn, since their schedules were so different from his.

After dressing, he made his way up to the galley and made coffee, leisurely enjoying a mug before setting out after sunrise. He was surprised when he went out on the side deck, as a thick fog had rolled in overnight. The sunrise was shrouded in a gray mist, and not really visible. For a moment he considered going back to bed, or at least in the salon, but the cool mist felt good on his face, and he decided to go ahead with his planned walk.

ACROSS THE BASIN, Baloney was waking up and was about to make a pot of coffee. He made it strong like he always did. There was nothing like a good caffeine jolt to start the day. He walked out the salon door and was hit with the same foggy surprise as Casey had been a few minutes before. The mist swirled around the dock light in the power pedestal behind his boat.

He carefully climbed the ladder to the flying bridge with one hand, while carrying the mug in his other. The rounded raw teak rungs got wetter as he ascended. His docksiders left dirty footprints on the polyurethane-painted deck. The dew was heavy back by the overhang where it was more open to the elements. Fortunately, his captain's chair had a cover, which was now dripping from the fog-driven dew.

He set his mug on the painted console next to the varnished teak control pod as he uncovered his dry chair. As he picked up his mug, he noticed it had left a water ring on the paint. Not that it mattered since he was going to have to dry everything with a chamois cloth after he was finished anyway.

Across the basin and through the fog, he thought he saw lights coming on *Epilogue*'s aft deck, meaning Sandy was up and about.

Casey's normal inspection went much slower than normal today, as he was hampered by the lack of sunlight. It would still be a couple of hours before the fog burned off. Though he liked watching the mist swirl around the boat barn's parking lot security lights. There was just enough light for him to safely cross over to the floating docks. There, the power pedestals still put out enough light to allow him to safely walk those docks.

As part of his walk, he checked to make certain the garbage cans had been emptied, that no faucets were dripping, and no shore cords or dock lines were left out where they might be a tripping hazard. Especially at night...or, in fog. He made a mental note of one dock light that was out. He'd tell Barry so he could get it fixed.

He found it ironic that he was now doing what Murph used to do when he worked for Casey. But Murph and Lindsay owned the majority of the *Mallard Cove* shares.

~

BIG LINCOLN WAS glad that his driver had suggested leaving early, as navigating the skiff in this fog had proven much more difficult than he'd bargained for. He had to go much slower than the Captain did. Fortunately, there was enough light coming from houses and docks that he was able to gauge how far he was off the shore. Only in a couple of places he couldn't see squat, and kept going by sticking to a compass direction.

The console only had two pull switches. The first one he tried turned on some electric motor in the back near the stern. The second had turned on the running lights and lit up the compass, the only instrument of any kind on the boat. The Captain hadn't been a big fan of putting money in gauges. Lincoln was glad that the man had at least sprung for the compass. Without it, he'd have been in big trouble off the dark stretch where *Southern Shores* had been supposed to have been built.

He managed to spot the center light on the span over the channel on the Fisherman Inlet Bridge. He knew to turn toward it and parallel the bottom of the Eastern Shore, just off *Mallard Cove*. After he passed that and made his turn back north, it got even trickier. He ran aground twice, but finally made it to the tug ten minutes late. The brothers weren't happy about that, and even less happy that the Captain wasn't here instead of him.

He grabbed the black backpack he'd found at the Captain's house that he used to move some of the money from the closet stash. He liked the bag so he had brought today's buy money in it.

"Yo, you wanna do bidness, or stan' out here gettin' all pissy an' stuff?"

Ben looked at Greg, both were still upset, but they both realized they might as well go ahead with this deal. They had the meth, and Big Lincoln had the cash. That's when Ben saw a small tear in Lincoln's backpack that had been crudely sewn up. He'd been the one who had sewn it up because this was the backpack he'd lost at that construction site. The bag of money for which the foreman had been murdered. They both knew about how the man had been brutally tortured before being killed, and Ben now figured that Big Lincoln had been the one who had done it.

In the spill from the tug's white anchor light, Greg saw that the color had drained out of Ben's face. He knew it had something to do with Lincoln, and he was now even more on guard. He saw Ben's hand start to move toward the gun that was under his shirt, and Greg shook his head slowly and emphatically, something not lost on Lincoln, who had brought his own concealed handgun to the party. He looked where Ben had been reaching when Greg waved him off and spotted the "print," or outline of Ben's gun. Now he correctly figured both brothers were armed. He motioned them into the wheelhouse to keep them together. He didn't want either of them to be able to flank him. Right now he wanted to get this deal done, and then get the hell out of there.

In the wheelhouse, he threw the backpack on the counter next to the bag of meth. "Here's yo money; take it out an' gimme the crystal."

Lincoln's hand now hovered by his own concealed gun, a move that wasn't lost on Greg as he spotted the gun's print. He also knew that a gunfight in these close quarters wouldn't be good, as there was no place to hide. Now the goal was to get out of here alive, but first, he wanted some answers.

Greg asked, "Where's the Captain?"

Lincoln had expected the question. "You don' need to worry 'bout him no more, you dealin' wit' me from now on."

Greg repeated his question, "Where is he?"

"I tol' you, he ain't nobody ya gotta worry 'bout. Now, let's get this done, I got a ways ta go in this fog."

Lincoln was beginning to get agitated, something neither of the brothers wanted to happen. Ben stepped up and transferred the money into a paper sack, then handed the empty backpack and the plastic bags of meth to Lincoln, who felt the weight before putting it in the backpack and zipping it shut.

"Back here on Friday, same time," Lincoln said.

Ben started to say something, but Greg cut him off, "Okay. Friday."

Lincoln backed out the door, untied, and then leaped into the skiff, dropping the backpack on the deck in the process. He started the motor and backed out into the darkness.

Back in the wheelhouse, the brothers waited until the sound of the old two-stroke faded in the distance before talking.

Ben said, "That's my backpack; the one that the site foreman swiped."

Greg asked, "Are you certain?"

"Yeah, I had ta stitch it up when it got ripped. So, Big Lincoln musta killed that man."

Greg nodded in agreement. "Likely. Also likely that the Captain is dead, too."

"What're we gonna do, Greg?"

"We are going home, tying up to the barge, then stripping it of everything we might need for the new business. Then we'll bring it out here, anchor it up, and blow it up tonight. This is the only place that he knows where to find us, and when he thinks we'll be here, and I intend on keeping it that way. But just in case, we are going to carry our pistols with us from now on. So, haul the anchor, and let's get out of here."

CASEY CONTINUED HIS INSPECTION WALK, one dock at a time. When he reached the center dock, he had a shock waiting for him. Halfway out, he spotted and recognized *Creola*. He saw that the cabin's hatch was open, and there was a dim light inside. He couldn't believe that Sally could be so brazen as to tie up here after the crap she tried to pull on them.

He went out on the finger pier, and quietly called out, "Sally!" But there was no response. He stepped over into the cockpit, and went to the door, again calling, "Sally!"

· · ·

SALLY SPOTTED someone coming down the floating dock, and the person paused behind *Creola*. In these low light conditions, she couldn't be certain, but she thought it was Casey. The person came down the finger pier between *Creola* and the boat she was on. Hearing him call out her name, she knew it was indeed Casey. When she didn't answer, she saw him go over to the open hatch and once again call out her name.

She stuck the gun out through the zippered opening in the canvas and isinglass as she activated the laser. At less than twenty feet, it would be an easy shot. She moved the dot of light up Casey's torso until she reached a spot halfway up his side. She squeezed the trigger, then heard him cry out before falling headfirst through the hatch, but then he quit making sounds.

She was surprised at how quiet the gun was, and the salesman had been right; it had almost no recoil. But now she had to act fast and get her boat out of there.

WHILE BIG LINCOLN had expected the brothers to be pissed off at no longer dealing with the Captain, he hadn't thought that both would be armed. He had wanted to tell them about increasing production, but instead, he'd just wanted to get out of there with his skin. Now he had to hurry to get back to the car, then he and his driver would go over to the brothers' house with their guns, and even odds.

Lincoln was again running faster than he should be, hitting yet another sandbar. But time was of the essence. He stuck closer to the western side of the channel and kicked on two motion-detecting lights at the seaplane ramp at C2. The fog was now in waves, with the occasional opening that lasted for a few seconds. He firewalled the throttle as he made the curve where *Mallard Cove* began.

Unfortunately, as he turned toward the Fisherman Inlet Bridge, he hit the thickest wave of fog yet, and he could barely see twenty feet in front of him. He had a split second of clarity when he saw the side of a white sailboat dead ahead, and the wide-open eyes of the woman at the helm. The bow of the deadrise hit right where she was, as it dug into and moved up the side, ripping the stern open.

The impact launched Big Lincoln out of the boat after he hit the small wood console, stunning and knocking the wind out of him. He sailed across what was left of the other boat's cockpit, landing in the water, struggling to stay afloat and catch his breath.

18

THE BIG SHOCK

Up on the flybridge of *Dorado*, Baloney was about to go below and get a coffee refill when he heard that two-stroke outboard coming down the ditch. Then one after the other, the pair of motion sensors kicked on the security lights over by the seaplane ramp as the boat passed by, a little too close to the shore. Baloney got a quick glimpse of the skiff before it disappeared back into the fog. He heard it blow past him at a much faster speed than it should in this dense mist.

He listened as it rounded the corner and headed for the bridge. That's when he heard the impact and the deathly silence that followed. Jumping out of his chair, he yelled across the basin, "Sandy! Did ya hear that?"

From over on Sandy's back deck he answered, "Yes! What do you think it was?"

"It was that damn idiot inna deadrise skiff! We gotta go and see if anybody got hurt. Getcher butt over here, pronto!"

Baloney started both engines and the generator, then he went down to the cockpit to unhook the shore power. He threw the stern line off just as Sandy arrived. He wasted no time, going straight to the remaining lines and casting those off as Baloney climbed back up on the flybridge.

Baloney raced out of *Casey's Cove*'s inlet as he turned on his big LED floodlights that illuminated the cockpit, then did the same for the ones that lit up the foredeck and the water beyond. He turned right and began looking for wreckage. A minute later, he spotted the mangled mess of lumber ahead. He spun *Dorado* around, sliding his cockpit up next to *Creola*'s with his transom backed up to what was left of the deadrise, which was still sticking out of the sailboat's cockpit. It didn't look like there was anyone inside of the open skiff. What was left of its smashed bow was now resting on the sailboat with the rest of the hull. For the moment, this was keeping the skiff from sinking.

The same couldn't be said about the sailboat. There was a body pinned under part of the skiff and the boat's partly missing stern was allowing water into the hull at an alarming rate.

Baloney turned on his VHF; "Mayday, mayday, mayday! Coast Guard, this is th' sportfish *Dorado*."

"*Dorado*, this is the Coast Guard on channel sixteen, what is the nature of your emergency?"

"Uh, Coast Guard, there's been ah collision between ah outboard an' ah sailboat jus' outside th' inlet at *Mallard Cove Marina*. Appears ta be at least one fatality. Th' sailboat is sinkin'. We're fixin' ta board an' search for survivors in th' cabin, over."

"*Dorado*, we are scrambling an RHIB to your location; ETA is twenty minutes. Do not board if the boat is sinking."

"Yeah well, this boat ain't got twenty minutes, an' if there's anybody inside, they ain't got that much time either. I'm goin' in."

"*Dorado*, negative. Stand down until the RHIB arrives!"

Baloney ignored the order and slid down the side pipes of the bridge ladder, telling Sandy to hold the two boats together as he leaped into the sailboat's now-flooding cockpit. A closer look at the woman confirmed his earlier thought, that she was indeed dead. Having never met Sally, he didn't recognize her. But even if he had known her, it still would have been tough to identify the body. Her face had borne a lot of the brunt of the original impact and was only partially intact. There didn't seem to be a way to free the body from under the skiff that had crushed her.

Instead, Baloney turned to the cabin and peered through the open hatch. That's when he received the shock of his life.

BIG LINCOLN WAS TREADING WATER, trying to get his bearings. He'd been thrown clear during the impact. He spotted the clearance light up on the bridge that he'd been heading for and now knew that *Mallard Cove* wasn't far away, to his right. He started swimming and reached the rocks of the jetty a couple of minutes later. He struggled to climb out on the slimy boulders. He reached the top just as what sounded like a big boat pulled up to the wreck.

The morning was still, and voices carried across the water. He heard one of them call the Coast Guard, who said they were on their way. Without a doubt, the cops would be next, and if they saw him dripping wet on the shore, they'd be quick to put two and two together. He had to get out of there and fast.

Fortunately, the cover on his phone was mostly waterproof and shock-resistant, and the phone still worked. He texted his driver to pick him up where they had been parked the other day. They still needed to get over to those two brothers' house and get control of things.

That's when he realized he'd left the backpack with the drugs in the skiff, that is, if it hadn't flown out in the crash. Not good, but there was nothing he could do about it now. He hurried down the dock toward the restaurant, then over by the boat barn to wait for his car. He'd check his gun when he got in the SUV, and change out the bullets for some dry ones, at the very least. So far, this had been a very expensive morning for him.

WHAT BALONEY HAD SEEN INSIDE WAS Casey, bound and gagged with duct tape, then wrapped up like a mummy in the near darkness, placed in a sitting position on the deck. The lights from *Dorado* barely reflected down into the cabin. His back was against the mast that ran through the deck and down to the keel, and the mummy wrap went around the mast as well. The water was already halfway up Casey's chest and rising fast. Baloney figured he had maybe a minute or two before the water would cover his head, if they had even that long.

Baloney took out his folding knife and cut through the side of the gag, along with the tape holding Casey's wrists together. Then he freed Casey's arms so that he could take his gag off. Meanwhile, he began feeling along the mast, cutting the tape as he went. He was hurrying because the water coming in had increased in volume as the cockpit had flooded, and that water was also cascading through the cabin hatch. They didn't have much time left. Thirty seconds later, it was almost up to Casey's nose, and he still wasn't freed from the mast.

"Bill, you've got to get out of there; she's on the verge of sinking!" Sandy's voice had a tinge of panic in it, and this was a first.

To reassure him, he called out, "Keep yer pants on, ya hack. One more minute."

Casey was trying to squirm and break the remaining bonds, but it was to no avail. "Get out of here, Bill!" With that last word, Casey sucked in a final breath as the water crested his nose.

"Yeah, yeah, yeah, like ya can tell me what ta do. Just hold that breath." He took in a big breath of his own, then ducked under the water to cut the last six inches of tape around the mast.

Once Casey felt that loosen, he twisted away from the mast and his face broke the surface. Gasping, he sucked in a breath.

"Case, ah hate ta rush ya, but we gotta get th' hell outta here! I ain't gonna die in a damn blow boat!" He shoved Casey toward the hatch, and the two climbed through, against the current from the water flooding the cabin.

Blinking in the bright lights from *Dorado*, that's when Casey saw Sally's body under the skiff. He turned away, then sloshed through the cockpit's water before scrambling up and over the gunwale of the big Merritt. Baloney was right behind him. Sandy helped both of them into the boat.

Sandy was floored. "What the hell were you doing on that boat, Casey?"

"My ex-wife abducted me, and she planned on drowning me out in the Atlantic. I recognized her boat, tied up over at *Mallard Cove*, which was the last place that it should've been. I climbed aboard to see if she was in the cabin when I was ambushed by a taser. I fell into the cabin, hitting the deck with my forehead, knocking me out cold.

"When I came to, I was bound and gagged and wrapped up tight against the mast. She was in front of me, ranting like a lunatic. I saw her go up and start the engine, still ranting, then we were underway. We hadn't been out two minutes before there was a loud crash, and I never heard her speak again."

Sandy asked, "What about the guy who was running the skiff?"

"Wasn't he in it?"

Baloney answered, "Nope. Nobody home."

"Then, I have no idea. I didn't hear anybody yelling for help."

Once again, Baloney climbed up to the flybridge and used the VHF.

"Coast Guard, sportfish *Dorado*."

"Fishing vessel *Dorado*, Coast Guard, go ahead."

"Ah, we confirmed at least one fatality, dunno about the captain uh th' skiff that hit th' sailboat, but we were able ta get inside th' cabin an' free ah hostage. We're gonna need some cops and medics ta check him out."

"*Dorado*, say again, you freed a *hostage*?"

"Roger, Coast Guard. He almost drowned, but ah got 'im outta there in time. He's in good shape, but needs checkin' out jus' in case."

"Roger that, *Dorado*. We will notify the local first responders. Can you stand by the area until the RHIB arrives on the scene?"

"Roger. We'll be standin' by."

∿

THE LINCOLN SUV came racing onto the brothers' property as they were emptying the last few things off the barge. Recognizing the vehicle, Greg shouted at Ben to cast off, as he ducked into the tugboat's wheelhouse and started the engine. Ben came racing back to the tug, as Lincoln leapt out of his vehicle with his gun raised, pointing at the tug as he raced down the dock.

Seeing the weapon pointed in his direction, Greg began firing. Caught in a no-man's land on the dock, Lincoln returned fire and raced down the dock. He headed for the barge, which was now about three feet away from the dock. Clearing the gap, he sought cover but only saw the shed to hide behind. Bullets began hitting the metal sides, as both brothers were shooting. Lincoln wondered where his driver was and why he wasn't shooting.

BACK IN THE SUV, Lincoln's driver watched as his boss jumped aboard the barge while taking fire. He briefly considered laying down suppression fire on the tugboat but realized he had less to cover himself than the brothers did. No sense in drawing their fire. If Big Lincoln lived through this, he'd just tell him his gun jammed. But if he didn't, then he would take over. If these guys weren't interested in doing business, and judging by the gunfire, they weren't, the driver still knew Lincoln's old producers and all of his distributors. He might not have enough to take over Fredericksburg, but he could handle Richmond.

PINNED down inside the shed as the barge was being towed, Lincoln spotted a manhole at the back. Looking for a safer refuge while he developed a plan, Lincoln ducked down into what he figured would be the bilge. Was he ever surprised to find the modern meth lab instead.

. . .

WITH NO MORE SHOTS FOR five minutes, Ben still kept an eye on the barge. He didn't believe that Lincoln had been killed, or even wounded, but he might be low or out of ammunition.

Greg took the tug's fire axe down from the holder on the bulkhead. They were approaching the end of the canal, and he pushed the throttle to the firewall. The old tug's engine labored at first, then relaxed a bit as it gained momentum with the barge.

Greg told Ben, "Get ready to cover me as I chop that polyethylene Hauser line in two. We'll let the barge's momentum carry it out in the middle, and we'll blow that thing."

"Wit' that guy still aboard?"

"You mean the guy who was shooting at us? Yes!"

Ben nodded, on board with the plan.

The aft wheelhouse window shattered as Lincoln got off a lucky shot. When no return fire came, he snuck a peek around the edge of the steel door. Two bullets hit the door, rattling him. He ran back to the manhole and ducked down into the lab. Once again, in the assumed safety of the lab, he briefly studied the equipment. Then he felt the movement of the barge change as it began to slow. He was curious about that, but then he spotted bottles filled with some type of gel that were taped to the sides of several of the fifty-five-gallon barrels. Leading into each container were a pair of wires that were attached to some type of remote light switch. At least, that's what it appeared to be. His eyes widened as he realized that this was explosives and the whole thing was rigged to blow. He started up the ladder when there was a blinding light.

Even though they were a good distance away from the barge, the tug was still rocked by the concussion from the blast. The force blew out the side, top, and bottom of the lab, and instantly pulverized Big Lincoln. What was left of the barge sank inside of a minute.

BACK AT MALLARD COVE, where Dorado had just arrived at the fuel dock with Casey, they heard but didn't feel the barge explosion. The deputy sheriff and the paramedics who were waiting on the dock all looked confused over the cause of the blast.

Baloney looked down from the flybridge and commented, "Sounds like youse guys are gonna have uh busy day."

"Maybe so," the deputy replied. "In the meantime, would you mind coming down and giving me a statement?" It was spoken more like a command than a question.

"Yeah, I would. Ya can either come up here an' I'll give it to ya, or ya can wait'll I'm done wit' this cigar. Ah can't come down there wit' it."

The deputy almost replied, but not before Casey put a hand on his arm. "Please let him finish his cigar. It's keeping a promise to his late wife."

The deputy looked confused for the second time in two minutes but then decided to take Sandy's statement while he waited for Baloney.

The paramedics checked Casey over but found nothing but a bump on his forehead, with no concussion, and two small puncture wounds on his side where the taser darts had lodged before Sally ripped them out.

After Baloney finally climbed down, he gave the deputy one flowery statement filled with "Baloneyisms" and a curse or three.

Murph and Lindsay had run over after hearing sirens. As they got past the privacy hedge, they were shocked to see all the emergency vehicles, with *Dorado* tied up at the fuel dock, swarming with first responders. After hearing Baloney's story, Lindsay ran back to get Dawn and then stayed with Summer while her mom was gone.

Dawn raced up, hugging Casey. "Are you all right, Case?"

"I'm fine, but Sally is dead. She was unhinged, acting like she'd had some kind of psychotic break. She blamed me for everything bad that ever happened to her. But I owe Baloney and Sandy my life. If he and Sandy had shown up a minute later, we wouldn't be having this conversation."

Sandy smiled. "Forget about it, Casey. I'm just happy we got to you when we did."

"Now hold on ah minute! 'We' got to him? Ah don't see your pants drippin', Hack!"

"Hey, I held the boat all by myself while you went swimming."

"Swimmin'! Are youse for real?"

Everyone on the dock who knew these two laughed. Once again, though, the paramedics and the deputy looked confused.

EPILOGUE

L ater that day, ten cases of Red Stripe beer arrived on a dolly
next to both Sandy's and Baloney's boats. There were notes on
each stating this was only a down payment on what they owed them,
and they were signed by both Casey and Dawn.

FINGERPRINTS TAKEN off the wheel and throttle of the skiff were
identified as belonging to one Herbert "Big Lincoln" Jackson. His
body was never recovered, and it was assumed that he drowned, and
his body swept out to sea. The drugs that were discovered aboard the
skiff were deemed to have been his and remain the largest confisca-
tion of meth by Northampton County to date.

Sally's body was recovered from the sunken sailboat by divers
later that day. One leg had gotten tangled in the sailboat's main sheet
line. Both boats were taken to Mockhorn Boat Works. *Creola* was
donated by Sally's sister, her only heir, to the waterman's fund run by
Rut Rutledge. After he finished repairing it, the fund auctioned it off,
with the proceeds going to several needy local families.

The skiff was found to have a phony registration and no title. Rut bought it from the county, intent on repairing it, and hanging a new four-stroke engine on the stern.

~

A MONTH LATER...

BALONEY SMILED as he watched a newer-looking crane and barge combination going up the ditch. The boom on the crane had signs proclaiming it to belong to Cleary Brothers Construction. While they didn't quite have enough to cover the cost of a new tugboat, with the business they were now bringing in, Greg figured they'd be able to afford it in less than a year. They already were awarded the contract to build the new boat ramp, fishing pier, and facilities for what was named the Betty Cooper Memorial Park. Baloney would be doing the ribbon cutting when it was finished.

~

LINCOLN'S DRIVER not only took over his organization, but his house as well, including his stash of cash. A month after that, his new Range Rover exploded, killing him instantly. The group that ran the Fredericksburg meth distribution took over Richmond the next day.

~

THREE MONTHS LATER...

CASEY, Dawn, Summer, Rikki, Cindy, Eric, Missy, and Candi returned to the dock on Sharke with a load of mahi and bluefish for the smoker. While they were grinning from ear to ear over their catch,

Lindsay and Murph were also grinning, waiting on the dock with an ultrasound photo. It turned out that their baby was instead *babies*, as in plural. A girl and a boy. Before Casey could threaten to evict them, Dawn suggested to him that they try for their own boy. Turnabout is fair play, so they say.

ABOUT MITIGATION BANKS

I didn't make up the concept, I stumbled across it in an Eastern Shore newspaper. A national conservation group had bought a soybean field in Northampton and created a mitigation bank to raise money by selling the credits. They had done so without the knowledge or approval of the Board of Supervisors, who were stunned and furious to discover neither was necessary by existing law. To their credit, they quickly passed an ordinance prohibiting any credits from being transferred out of the county.

Before the passing of the new ordinance, in addition to Northampton County, any of those credits could be used in Accormack County as well as portions of Virginia Beach. Meaning Northampton would lose valuable and productive farmland while other counties would have their tax base enriched at the expense of Northampton residents.

Mark this as being one of those truths that are stranger than fiction.

GLOSSARY

I grew up on the water in South Florida, and I have an extensive boating background. I've worked on boats, built them, re-built them, and spent a good amount of time in boatyards. I've always loved boats, and ever since I was a pre-teenager, I haven't gone longer than six months without owning at least one. Most of my friends are boaters, too. So it's easy for me to forget that not everyone is as familiar with the jargon as my friends and me, which is something that I've now been reminded of on more than one occasion. (My apologies to those readers that I ended up sending to the dictionary!) To make amends, here's a (growing) list of uniquely nautical terms from several of my books. Bear in mind that these definitions are based on my own usage and experience. Things can be different from one region to another. For instance, you can fish for stripers in Montauk, New York, but here in Virginia, we fish for rockfish. But the true name for the target species is "striped bass."

So, here are the definitions of some of the more confusing words, at least as I know them. We'll start with a half dozen simple ones, then move on to those that are more complex:

- **Bow:** the front of the boat.

- **Stern:** back of the boat.
- **Port:** the left side of the boat.
- **Starboard:** the right side of the boat.
- **Aft:** the rear of the boat.
- **Forward:** (fore) the front of the boat.
- **Bulkhead:** boat wall.
- **Center Console:** a type of boat with a raised helm console in the middle of the boat with space on each side to walk around. Most also incorporate a built-in bench seat or cooler seat in the front.
- **Chine:** the longitudinal area running fore and aft where the bottom meets the side. It can be rounded or "sharp." They hurt when the boat rocks and it meets your head when you are swimming next to it. Trust me on that.
- **Citation:** at an airport, it's a type of jet made by Cessna. But here in Virginia, it's a slip of paper suitable for framing, issued by the state confirming that you caught a fish that's considered large for its particular species. Or it can be a speeding ticket, either on water or land. I like the fish kind better.
- **Covering Board:** a flat surface at the top of a gunwale usually made out of teak or fiberglass, that's used as a step for boarding and for mounting recessed rod holders.
- **Deck:** what floors on boats are called.
- **Fighting Chair:** a specialized chair that can be turned to face a fish. Mounted on a sturdy stanchion with a built-in gimbal, the chair allows the angler to use the attached footrest to use their legs and body to gain more leverage on a large fish. Most of today's fighting chairs are based on the design by my late friend John Rybovich.
- **Fish Box:** a built-in storage box for the day's catch. They can be either elevated in the stern, or in the deck with a flush-mounted lid. Some of the higher-end sportfish boats

have cooling systems or automatic ice makers that continually add ice throughout the trip.

- **Fishing Cockpit:** the lower aft deck on a sport fisherman that usually contains a fighting chair, fish box, baitwell, and tackle center. Surrounded on three sides by the gunwales and the stern. The cockpit deck is usually just above the waterline, with scuppers that drain overboard. Can get flooded when backing down hard on a big fish.
- **Flying Bridge (Flybridge):** a permanently mounted helm area on top of the wheelhouse. Can be open or enclosed.
- **Following Sea:** when the waves are moving toward the boat from behind the stern.
- **Gaff:** a large, usually barbless hook at the end of a pole, used for landing fish. They come in different sizes and lengths.
- **Gangway (Gangplank):** a removable ramp or set of stairs attached to the side of larger boats to allow easier access for boarding from a dock. Usually hinged to allow for tide variation.
- **Gear:** marine transmission which has forward, neutral, and reverse.
- **Gimbal:** there are a few types, but the ones in my books are rod holders with swivels built into fighting chairs and fishing belts.
- **Gunwale (pronounced gun-nul):** aft side area of a boat above the waterline, also the area on either side of a fishing cockpit.
- **Hatch:** a hole in a deck or bulkhead with a cover that may be hinged or completely removable. On a sport fisherman, the door into the wheelhouse may be called either a hatch or a door.
- **Head:** a bathroom, or a marine toilet.
- **Helm:** the area that includes the steering and engine controls. In many sportfishing boats, the controls are

mounted on a helm pod, a wood box with radiused edges that juts out of a cabinet or bulkhead.

- **Lean Seat:** a high bench seat usually found behind the helm of a center console. Designed to be leaned against or sat upon. May have storage built-in under the seat section.
- **Mezzanine Deck:** a shallow, raised deck on a sportfish just forward of the fishing cockpit, and aft of the wheelhouse bulkhead. Usually contains aft-facing bench seating for anglers to comfortably watch the baits that are being trolled behind the boat.
- **Outriggers:** long aluminum poles on sportfishing boats that are raked up and aft from up alongside the wheelhouse. They are extended outward when fishing, having clips on lines that carry the fishing lines out away from the boat, creating a wider spread.
- **Rod Holder:** As the name suggests, a device that a fishing rod butt is inserted into to hold it steady. There are recessed types that are mounted on covering boards, and exposed ones attached to railings or tower legs.
- **Salon:** a living room area of a boat's cabin.
- **Scuppers:** deck or cockpit drains.
- **SeaKeeper Gyro:** a stabilizing gyro that almost eliminates roll in boats.
- **Shaft:** attaches a propeller to the gear.
- **Sheer Line:** the rail edge where the foredeck meets the side of the hull.
- **Sonar/Fish Finder:** electronic underwater 'radar' that displays the sea floor, and anything between it and the boat.
- **Sportfisherman (Sportfish):** a unique style of boat designed specifically for fishing.
- **Stem:** the forwardmost edge of the bow.
- **Stern:** the farthest aft part of the boat, also called the transom.

- **Tackle Center:** a cabinet in the fishing cockpit or the center console that holds hooks, swivels, leads, and other fishing supplies.
- **(Tuna) Tower:** an aluminum pipe structure located above the house or the flybridge designed to hold spotters or riders and may or may not have an additional helm.
- **Transom:** stern.
- **Transom (Tuna) Door:** a door in the stern just above the waterline, designed for boating large fish but is also useful for retrieving swimmers and divers.
- **Trough:** the lowest point between waves.
- **Wheel (Propeller):** slang for a prop.
- **Wheel (Steering):** controls the boat's direction.
- **Wheelhouse (House):** the cabin section of a boat, which sometimes contains an enclosed helm.

ABOUT THE AUTHOR

Don Rich is the author of the bestselling Coastal Adventure, Coastal Beginnings, and Mobjack Mysteries series. Don's books are set mainly in the mid-Atlantic because of his love for this stretch of coastline.

As a fifth-generation Florida native who grew up on the water, he has spent a good portion of his life on, in, under, or beside it. He now makes his home in central Virginia. When he's not writing or watching another fantastic mid-Atlantic sunset, he can often be found in a marina or boatyard somewhere around the Chesapeake Bay or the Atlantic, researching his next book.

Don loves to hear from readers, and you can reach him via email at contact@donrichbooks.com

 X

ALSO BY DON RICH

Please check my website www.DonRichBooks.com for a current list of all my book titles.

The Coastal Beginnings Series:

(The prelude to the Coastal Adventure Series)

- COASTAL CHANGES
- COASTAL TREASURE
- COASTAL RULES
- COASTAL BLUFFS

The Coastal Adventure Series:

- COASTAL CONSPIRACY
- COASTAL COUSINS
- COASTAL PAYBACKS
- COASTAL TUNA
- COASTAL CATS
- COASTAL CAPER
- COASTAL CULPRIT
- COASTAL CURSE
- COASTAL JURY
- COASTAL CURRENCY
- COASTAL CRUISE

The Mobjack Mysteries Series:

- Mobjack Gamble

Other Books by Don Rich:

- GhostWRITER

Here's A Tropical Authors Novella by Deborah Brown, Nicholas Harvey,

and Don Rich:

- **Priceless**

Go to my website at www.DonRichBooks.com for more information about joining my **Reader's Group**! And you can follow me on Facebook at: https://www.facebook.com/DonRichBooks

I'm also a member of TropicalAuthors.com, where you can find my latest books and those by dozens of my coastal writer friends!

www.ingramcontent.com/pod-product-compliance
Lightning Source LLC
Chambersburg PA
CBHW071356120626
46546CB00002B/720